The God I Know...
and the Relationship
We Need

Steve White and Joyce Hill

RIVER BIRCH PRESS

Daphne, Alabama

The God I Know...and the Relationship We Need
by Steve White and Joyce Hill
Copyright ©2021 Steve White and Joyce Hill

Unless otherwise identified, Scripture is taken from: *THE HOLY BIBLE: New International Version* ©1978 by the New York International Bible Society, used by permission of Zondervan Bible Publishers.

Scriptures marked NASB are taken from the *New American Standard Bible*, Copyright ©1960, 1962, 1963, 1968, 1971, 1973, 1975, 1977 by The Lockman Foundation.

ISBN 978-1-951561-68-0 (print)
ISBN 978-1-951561-69-7 (e-book)

For Worldwide Distribution
Printed in the U.S.A.

River Birch Press
P.O. Box 868, Daphne, AL 36526

For Sherrie and Peter

To God be the glory!

Joyce and I wrote this book with the hope maybe one person would see God more clearly and that it would change their life. We hope you're that person!

Table of Contents

Foreword

Joyce and I have prayed many times about who we could get to endorse our book and write a foreword. Typically, you look for very popular people in the Christian community with name recognition, a great platform, and millions of followers on social media. One night I was praying about an endorsement and God whispered to me, "I endorse your book."

And that's all we needed. It gave us both a sense of having done His will by writing this book. It really doesn't matter now how God uses the book. We know we have been obedient to His leading and that He endorses it!

In Hebrews 12:2, the writer states that we should fix our eyes on Jesus, the Author and Perfecter of our faith, who for the joy set before Him endured the cross, despising the shame, and has sat down at the right hand of the throne of God.

As this book has been dedicated to the glory of God, Joyce and I give thanks to the Lord for His inspiration through the Holy Spirit! His endorsement is the one that counts, not the endorsement of man.

We are so thankful and grateful for His endorsement:

I approve this message.

—*God*

Preface

We live in very difficult times. There is great division in America and the world. The major areas of division include race, gender, politics, age, and economics. We have lost the ability or desire to respectfully disagree. All in all, we have ignored God's law to "love thy neighbor as thyself" and have stooped to name calling and abuse.

In the following pages of this book, you will find the authors invite you to the understanding that life is not easy for any of us. We all suffer hardship and tragedy and loss of loved ones, but with the love of our Father God, much beauty and joy can also be experienced. It is important to minister to one another, reflecting the love of God and offering each other encouragement.

We are all ONE in the Lord. There is no greater number than one. When we accept the Lord as our Savior, we become one with Him. We all have our life stories to tell, and when we do, we come to the realization we are no different from each other. We were all created equal by God in His image, so how could we not be one? When we realize we all have experiences with some of the same or similar problems and issues, we can feel some affinity with each other.

Our commitment in life is not to condemn one another but to guide, encourage, advise (when necessary), and love our brothers and sisters. We can help them overcome what tends to discourage them so they can experience the joy of the gift of life.

Since we are one in the Lord and children of our heavenly Father, we therefore are brothers and sister to each other. Our mission in life is to encourage one another, especially those who are downtrodden or in the grip of despair. We need to realize we are servants to our brothers and our sisters as Christ was a servant to those who came to Him.

When we study biblical Hebrew, we learn there is no such thing as an evil man—only a man evil. As Jonathan Cahn explains in his *Book of Mysteries*, man is the creation of God with free will and may choose to be good or evil. Therefore, in Hebrew, the adjective comes after the man who is created by God—man good or man evil.

We must never be ashamed of who we are because this would only be an insult to the One who created us. We may not be proud of some of the things we have done in our lives, but we must recognize when we have strayed from His will that we can be forgiven and correct those misdeeds. We also know our heavenly Father is merciful, and by His grace, He loves us and will never abandon us.

It is the hope and prayer of the authors of this book that when you have read it and meditated upon it, you will all be encouraged to become ONE in the Lord.

—*Peter Hill*

Acknowledgments

Steve: First, I would like to thank my co-author Joyce Hill for her writing, spiritual insights, and prayer support while writing this book. Joyce and I went to high school together where we hardly knew each other. Somehow we connected on Facebook over fifty years later. As we chatted, it became apparent we had both been saved since we had last seen each other. She read my first book *Please Change Your Mind* and liked it. She asked me if I had any ideas about new books and I told her about my idea for The Truth About God and the Revival We Need. I suggested she co-author the book with me and she agreed.

We wrote chapters of the book independently and edited each other's work. We have recently reunited in person in late August 2020. I believe this book came about through Divine intervention. High school friends connecting on social media for the first time in 55 years; discovering they shared a Savior; and agreeing to write a book together—that just doesn't happen. Yet, God made it so, and to Him be the glory!!

I would also like to thank my wife Sherrie for her support. She edited much of the work and made it better. She has also been a great comfort and companion during my illness. She has always been a real blessing to me and I thank God for her.

And I want to thank my Lord. He gave me the idea and the inspiration for this book. He led me to Joyce, He led me to our agent Keith Carroll and and led us to Brian Banashak of River Birch Press as our publisher. Without Him none of this would have happened. I pray the readers of *The God I Know and the Relationship We Need* will be blessed, and my Lord and Savior Jesus Christ will be glorified!!

Joyce: My college degree is in Journalism, back when it was considered an honorable career, but I could never have done this without Steve's faith in God and in me as a new author. Thank you,

Steve! The most surprising aspect of writing this book is many chapters seemed almost effortless to write. Both Steve and I would wake up in the morning and start to write about what God gave us in our dreams. We would edit each other's work, and the result was an incredible blending of our writing styles into one complete effort! (By the way, Steve lives in Atlanta, Georgia, and I live in Lancaster County, Pennsylvania!)

I have depended on my loving husband, Peter, in my learning curve of how to write a book. He has been my chief cheerleader and encourager as well as contributing wonderful insights into each topic I tackled. (He also wrote the Preface in this book.) His love and prayers have been my mainstay in this project.

I truly appreciate the patience and professionalism of our literary agent, Keith Carroll, and thank him for guiding us in the right direction in our rewriting. God gave us Brian Banashak of River Birch Press as our publisher, and he has guided us smoothly through the publishing process. I also want to thank Rev. Keith Almond and Rev. Jim Ferguson for their attention to the details of the Bible scriptures we used. Thanks to Jane Campbell, professional editor, for her insights and suggestions, as well as Kathy Bowman, Music Director of the National Christian Choir, for her insights and endorsement. Also, I give many thanks to my friends—Sue and Gerry Edwards, Bing and Jackie Fuller, Bill and Rhonda Watkins, and others—who supported the writing of this book with their love, prayers, encouragement, and suggestions.

But, most of all, I thank my Lord and Savior, Jesus Christ, for the vision and inspiration to accomplish this work of love! To God be the glory for the things He has done. May this book help to bring new believers into the Kingdom of God!

Introduction

When I was growing up, whenever I got in trouble my father would always say, "I'm so disappointed in you." He was always disappointed in something—my report card, my behavior, my attitude, something. But what I heard was not what he said. What I heard was, "You are a disappointment."

Over time I came to believe that I was a disappointment. In reality, what he really meant was that he was disappointed in what I did or what I said. He never explained to me that being disappointed in my behavior was different than being disappointed in me. He could have said, "I don't like what you did, but I love you." But he didn't.

I realize now, of course, he did love me. But by then, the damage was done. When you believe you are a disappointment, it becomes a self-fulfilling prophecy. If you believe your core essence is a disappointment, then of course you're going to be a disappointment in marriage, in parenting, at work, everywhere. And so, naturally I was.

Believing you are a disappointment carries over into love. Nobody loves a disappointment, so love must therefore be conditional. When you are good (and not a disappointment), then you are loved. But when you are a disappointment, you believe that love is certainly withheld. So, I traded all my pre-teen years for being a "good boy." As a teen, however, I became very rebellious. Why not? If you already know you're a disappointment, then go for the gusto. I became what I heard—I was a disappointment.

My wife, Sherrie, as a little girl, once overheard her mother say to her aunt, "Well, at least she's pretty." But what Sherrie heard was, "I'm not very smart." And she believed it for a long time. What people say is not always what we hear.

When you're continually told you are fat, dumb, ugly, or whatever, pretty soon you begin to believe it's true. As a result, many of us walk around believing something that isn't true. Sometimes we learn the truth from experience—like fire is hot. Sometimes we believe things our parents tell us are true. Or in many cases, discouraging words could come from a teacher, a coach, a mentor, a brother or sister, or someone we really trust. We then embark on life believing what we heard, not necessarily what was said, or even what was actually true.

I saw a video of Nicole Johnson speaking to an audience about walking into her den and asking her children to turn down the TV. No one responded, so she said it again louder. When no one responded, she finally had to go turn it down herself. Then she noticed it in other places.

She was at a party with her husband, and it was time to leave. She walked over to him, and he was talking with a friend and kept right on talking. He didn't even turn toward her. Then, it came to her, "He can't see me. I'm invisible." Then she noticed it other places. She was walking her son to school and his teacher said, "Who is that with you today, Jake?" And he said, "Nobody."

Later, she was at a party for a friend that was returning home from a trip to England. Her friend gave her a book about the great cathedrals of Europe. Inside her friend had written an inscription, "With admiration for the greatness you are building when no one sees." She saw that many of the great cathedrals took over a hundred years to complete—more than one working man's lifetime—and the builders received no credit. The inscriptions on the cathedrals simply read, "Builder Unknown."

One story in the book caught her eye about a builder who was carving a bird into a beam that would be covered up by the roof. When asked why he was doing something no one would ever see, he replied, "Because God sees." She said in that moment it was as if God whispered to her, "I see you. You're not invisible to Me." She knew then that nothing was too small for Him to notice. God saw every sequin she sewed, every cupcake she baked, every load of wash she did, and every sacrifice she made.

She went on to say that when her son invites a college friend home for Thanksgiving she doesn't want him say, "You're not going believe my mom. She gets up at 4:00 a.m., she bakes pies, and bastes the turkey, irons the napkins, and sets the table. She's just incredible." She said she didn't want him to say those things. She just wanted him to desire to come home. And she wanted her son to tell his friend, "You're going to love it there." She realized that she too was building a cathedral of her own. And she wasn't doing it for them; she was doing it for Him.

I cried for a long time after that video ended. I cried because I heard God whisper to me, "You're not a disappointment to me!"

I don't know what you believe about yourself or why or how you came to believe it. I just know that sometimes what we hear is not what was said. I also don't know what you believe about God or how or why you came to believe it. But we all owe it to ourselves to make sure whatever we believe is really true.

I told God I had read the Bible and that I knew a lot about Him and who He was. Then I asked, "But God, who am I?" And He said, "You are Mine" (Isaiah 43:1). Reflect on these words for a moment:

You say I am loved, when I don't feel a thing,
You say I am strong, when I think I am weak,
You say I am held, when I am falling short,
When I don't belong, You tell me I am Yours,
And I believe.

The God I know is worth knowing. And what He thinks about you is worth knowing. In the following chapters, Joyce and I want to share Him with you, and what He thinks about you. Better hold on tight, because He is gonna rock your world!

—Steve White, 2021

1

The Best Picture of God

One of my favorite writers is James Michener. His most famous book is probably *Hawaii,* which was published in 1959, not coincidentally the year Hawaii became our 50th state. He painted pictures with words. It took him five pages to describe a sunset. As a result, you could just see it in your mind's eye.

My favorite Michener book was *Chesapeake.* I grew up in Maryland and was very familiar with the Chesapeake Bay area. My father's family was from Crisfield, Maryland, and they were all watermen who had large crab and oyster commercial businesses. Many of the scenes he described in that book painted vivid memories of things I had actually seen. He created visuals with words.

There is no greater visual in the Bible of God's character, attitude, and personality than the parable of the Prodigal Son. That parable in Luke 15 tells us so much about who God is and what He is like. In that story, God is the symbolic father of the prodigal son. And that is perhaps the best context from which to view everything about God—as a loving Father.

It is no irony Jesus is the one telling this parable. He was talking about His own Father, and no one knew Him better. So, Jesus tells us this story about His Father:

Jesus continued: "There was a man who had two sons. The younger one said to his father, 'Father, give me my share of the estate.' So he divided his property between

1

them.

"Not long after that, the younger son got together all he had, set off for a distant country and there squandered his wealth in wild living. After he had spent everything, there was a severe famine in that whole country, and he began to be in need. So he went and hired himself out to a citizen of that country, who sent him to his fields to feed pigs. He longed to fill his stomach with the pods that the pigs were eating, but no one gave him anything.

"When he came to his senses, he said, 'How many of my father's hired servants have food to spare, and here I am starving to death! I will set out and go back to my father and say to him: Father, I have sinned against heaven and against you. I am no longer worthy to be called your son; make me like one of your hired servants.' So he got up and went to his father. But while he was still a long way off, his father saw him and was filled with compassion for him; he ran to his son, threw his arms around him and kissed him.

"The son said to him, 'Father, I have sinned against heaven and against you. I am no longer worthy to be called your son.'

"But the father said to his servants, 'Quick! Bring the best robe and put it on him. Put a ring on his finger and sandals on his feet. Bring the fattened calf and kill it. Let's have a feast and celebrate. For this son of mine was dead and is alive again; he was lost and is found.' So, they began to celebrate (Luke 15:11-24).

In verse 11, the younger son wanted his inheritance right now. He didn't want to wait. In essence, he was saying, "Dad, I wish you were dead so I could get my half of the inheritance now!" The father didn't argue, he didn't ask any questions, and he didn't try to talk him out of it. Nor did he tell him how disappointed he was in his son's decision. This father let his son exercise his free will—just the way God does.

The son clearly believed, "It's all about me." So, as the story goes, he took the money, left home, and went on his way. It was time for wine, women, and song! The Bible calls it "wild living." He enjoyed the modern-day notion of strip clubs, bars, massage parlors, gambling, and anything else he wanted to do until the money ran out, and the famine came! Then the son became needy, certainly not the result he had hoped to create.

So, the younger son took a job feeding pigs, which is significant because Jewish law (the laws of Moses) said that pigs were unclean and forbids Jews to eat pigs or even offer pigs as sacrifices. Jews were not even allowed to touch pigs! For this son to consider eating the food that pigs had touched meant he had degraded himself beyond belief. He had sunk to the lowest depths. No one gave him anything to eat, and that is when he began to change what he believed.

The parable says, "He came to his senses," which means he began to think differently. He remembered that his father's servants ate better than he was eating. When he thought differently, he began to feel differently. His belief that "It's all about me" suddenly changed to "It's all about Dad." He now felt remorse. And when he felt differently, he did something different—he decided to go back home!

Not only did the son realize what he had to do, but he also knew what he had to say to his father, "Dad, I have sinned against you and heaven. I'm not worthy to be your son. Please let me be one of your servants." His apology seems to reflect a broken and contrite heart. So the son decided what he had to do and say to his father, and then he did it. He didn't just think about doing it; he did it.

The son went home, probably dreading seeing his father again.

He was sure he would hear a few "I told you so's," along with maybe even one, "I'm so disappointed in you." The father saw him when he was a great way off. Maybe the son was at the end of a long dirt driveway. Maybe the father was on his front porch in his rocking chair. Maybe he was thinking it might be his son, so he took out his binoculars and confirmed it was indeed his son. What did the father do? What would you do if this was your son?

In all honesty, if it were my son, what I would probably say is, "Well, look who's come home. Did you enjoy yourself? You are in soooooooo much trouble. You go to your room and stay there until you are fifty. There will be no electronics, no car privileges, and no TV. Now get out of my sight, I don't even want to see you. You are such a disappointment."

But fortunately, the father in this story is a symbol of God Himself and not me or my earthly dad. The Father isn't mad. He is filled with compassion. COMPASSION! He loves His son so much that love is all He feels. He has been grieving the loss of His son. And all He cares about is that he is home. So what does the Father do? He RUNS to His son. This is the only place in the Bible I know that depicts God in a hurry. When one of God's children decides to return home, this is how God responds. He will have compassion, and He will run to you!

I don't know where you might be in your life right now. Maybe you've been away from God for a long time; maybe there was a betrayal, a bankruptcy, a divorce, a prolonged illness, or maybe the loss of a loved one. Or maybe you're just tired of eating pig slop like the young son in the story. But if you can change what you believe, as the son did in this story, then things will change for you as they did for him.

All I know is when you decide to come back to God, He will have compassion, and He will run to you. That is the God I know. I've wept in His embrace. When I thought I wasn't loved, He showed me what love really is.

Picture the father running down the long dirt driveway to meet his son. What did he do? He threw his arms around him and kissed him! Can you imagine what the son was thinking? This was the last thing he had expected. So he started to tell his father what he decided to say when he was back in that pigsty. He repeated it verbatim. But the father wasn't even listening. The father was shouting instructions to his servants, "Quick! Bring the best robe and put it on him. Put a ring on his finger and sandals on his feet. Bring the fattened calf and kill it. Let's have a feast and celebrate."

The father was so excited to have his son back home that he was shouting instructions to his servants. (An interesting side note is that the ring put on his finger was technically a symbol of authority/full son-ship and, therefore, an expression of the father's love!). The father wasn't listening to the son's apology because he'd already heard it.

When the son was a great way off, he wasn't at the end of the driveway. The great way off was the pigsty when the son said it the first time. God sees you wherever you are. However far away you might think you are—God sees you there, and God hears you there.

The father didn't have time to listen to an apology he had already heard. He was busy planning the celebration. And look what he had in mind—the best robe, a ring for his finger, sandals for his feet, and the fattened calf. This event called for a celebration—the best of everything!

No differently, this is what God has for you when you return to Him. Can you even imagine a father who loves you this much? He wants the best of everything for you! In His mind, returning to Him is a cause for celebration, not chastisement that you might expect, but a celebration. That is how much He loves you! He sees your returning as an event worth celebrating.

In my opinion, the story of the Prodigal Son is the happiest story in the Bible. It's a story that paints such a beautiful picture of God's love, compassion, wanting to celebrate your return home by giving you the best of everything. Anyone who changes what they think and decides to return to God will be treated the way this prodigal son was treated. It doesn't get any happier than that for me.

FOR PERSONAL REFLECTION AND DISCUSSION

- From the Prodigal Son story, what did you learn about God's character?
- Why do you think the father was in a hurry to run to his son?
- Why was the son's confession so important? Why is confession important to you?

2

The Key Is Relationship

When I had my consulting business, I was the primary salesperson, the "rainmaker," as they used to say. As the business grew, I needed others to step up and begin bringing in their own business, but they needed training on how to be a good salesperson. Today there are thousands of books, videos, seminars, and workshops that can teach you how to do so.

In my experience, the key to my sales success was the relationship I had with my clients. If they trusted me to tell them the truth (even if it hurt), give them a fair price, deliver a quality product, and really listen to their needs and problems, then we had a good relationship, and they would be inclined to do more business with me. The best source of new business is always a satisfied old client. If you have that kind of relationship with your customers, you will be successful. The same is true with God. It's all about having a good relationship with Him.

Too many Christian people today are just focused on *doing* things the best way they can. They are sincere and mean well, and they are engaged in many good, positive activities. Some are busy *doing* things because they think that's what good Christians should do. Others are doing things because they believe it is pleasing to God. And some are doing things because they think it earns them favor with God.

But here is the truth—God doesn't need or want you to do anything! He wants to have a relationship with you. That relationship may lead to *doing* many things, but the relationship comes first and is the *basis* for all the doing. The doing is something that comes out of the relationship.

God's reality is this: "Be still and know that I am God" (Psalm 46:10). Being (who you are) comes before doing (things you do because of who you are). God wants you to *be* something before He wants you to *do* something. Jesus said, "Love the Lord your God with all your heart, mind, soul, and strength. And love your neighbor as yourself." He told us about loving but didn't say anything about doing!

God wants a love relationship with you. He wants to be the Love of your life. He wants to walk with you every minute of every day and enjoy unbroken fellowship with you. He wants to give you the desires of your heart. You are not your own; you were bought and paid for—the price was Jesus' death on the cross.

God loves you so much, and the sacrifice of Jesus allowed you to be reconciled to Him. He loved you so much that He chose to die rather than live without you. Christianity is not about performance (*doing*); it is about relationship (*being*). God wants you to *be* with Him before you *do* for Him!

The Old Testament prophet, Micah, gave us a simple formula for what God wants for us. "He has told you, O Man, what is good; and what does the Lord require of you but to do justice, to love kindness, and to walk humbly with your God" (Micah 6:8). So how can we do all that when God is in heaven, and we are on earth? Easy—we focus on our relationship with God and listen to Him.

In Luke 10:39-42, as Jesus was visiting Martha and Mary and Lazarus, Martha was doing all the work to prepare dinner. She saw Mary sitting at the feet of Jesus, listening to Him. Martha went to Jesus and asked Him to send Mary into the kitchen to help (*doing*). But He answered that "Mary has chosen the good part, which shall not be taken from her" (*being*)! Martha was *doing* for Jesus, while Mary was *being* with Jesus. Mary was focused on her relationship with Jesus.

As part of learning about our new relationship in Christ, we need to let the Holy Spirit teach us God's ways. Joshua 1:9 states that he (Joshua) has commanded you to be strong and courageous and not afraid or discouraged for the Lord your God is with you wherever you go. Hebrews 1:9 tells us that "You have loved righteousness and hated lawlessness; therefore, God, your God, has anointed you with the oil of gladness above your companions."

Furthermore, Paul encourages us to "Let the word of Christ richly dwell within you, with all wisdom teaching and admonishing one another with psalms and hymns and spiritual songs, singing with thankfulness in your hearts to God" (Colossians 3:16). Another way of being is to be anxious for nothing, but in everything by prayer and supplication with thanksgiving, let your requests be made known to God (Philippians 4:6). God's lifetime courses at Holy Spirit University, aka, the Bible, will teach you all about being so you can teach others!

When I think about my relationship with God, I always think about the thief on the cross. Luke tells the story in chapter 23, verses 39-43. Jesus was crucified between two thieves. The crowds were around, and the soldiers were mocking Jesus.

Then one of the thieves says to Jesus, "Aren't you the Messiah? Save yourself, and us!" Then the other criminal rebukes him and says, "Don't you fear God, since you are under the same sentence? We are being punished justly, and getting what our deeds deserve. But this man (Jesus) has done nothing wrong."

How did this thief know Jesus had done nothing wrong? Perhaps he had heard Jesus preach to the crowds earlier. Perhaps he was one of the 5,000 Jesus had fed. Or perhaps he was just listening to the crowds around the cross. The Bible doesn't give us an answer. But it is clear that this thief saw something in Jesus that attracted him.

The thief then turned to Jesus and said, "Jesus, remember me when you come into your kingdom." He knew Jesus' name! He knew Jesus was about to die, and whatever kingdom Jesus was about to enter, it wasn't going to be a kingdom on earth. Jesus replied, "Truly I tell you, today you will be in Paradise."

So, this thief on the cross was going to enter Jesus' kingdom that day—not tomorrow, but that day! So, what did this thief ever *do* for Jesus? Absolutely nothing! But for the briefest of moments, he had a relationship with Jesus. And that relationship meant everything! That relationship resulted in being with Jesus in Paradise.

The thief was never baptized, never took communion, never taught Sunday school, never went to a prayer meeting, never tithed, and never did *anything*! And yet we know he is with Jesus at this very moment. The relationship meant everything; deeds meant nothing.

Jesus said, "Seek first the kingdom of God and all these things will be added unto you" (Matthew 6:33). And if I seek first a relationship with God, there will be plenty of time to do things later. So, don't "*do* your best" just "*be* your best." It's all about the relationship. And by His grace, you can do it!

FOR PERSONAL REFLECTION AND DISCUSSION

- What does God expect of you?
- What does God's love require of you?
- In twenty-five words or less, describe your relationship with God.

3

The Hiding Place

As a rebellious teenager, I always tried to hide the bad stuff I was doing from my parents. I used to steal my mom's cigarettes, but eventually, I started buying my own. I would try and hide them in my room, but somehow, she always found them. When I'd have a few beers with my friends and come home late, I would try and hide the fact I'd been drinking.

One night I'd had a few too many, and I guess I was a little loud trying to sneak in after curfew and woke them up. I think it was my dad, and he wanted to be disappointed again. I was sooooo busted! If you can't hide things from your mom and dad, think how hard it is to hide things from God. He is ever-present and all-knowing so you can't hide anything from Him. The following story is a good example.

In that place between wakefulness and dreams, I found myself in a room. There were no distinguishing features except for the one wall covered with small index card files. They were like the ones in libraries that list titles by author or subject in alphabetical order. But these files, which stretched from floor to ceiling and seemingly endless in either direction, had very different headings.

As I drew near the wall of files, the first to catch my attention was one that read "Girls I have liked." I opened it and began flipping through the cards. I quickly shut it, shocked to realize that I recognized the names written on each one. And then, without being told, I knew exactly where I was.

This lifeless room with its small files contained a crude catalog

11

system for my life with the actions of my every moment, big and small, written in a detail my memory couldn't match. A sense of wonder and curiosity, coupled with horror, stirred within me as I began randomly opening files and exploring their content. Some brought joy and sweet memories, others a sense of shame and regret so intense that I would look over my shoulder to see if anyone was watching.

A file named "Friends" was next to one marked "Friends I have betrayed." The titles ranged from the mundane to the outright weird. "Books I Have Read," "Lies I Have Told," "Comfort I Have Given," "Jokes I Have Laughed At." Some were almost hilarious in their exactness: "Things I've yelled at my brothers." Others I couldn't laugh at: "Things I Have Done in My Anger," "Things I Have Muttered Under My Breath at My Parents."

I never ceased to be surprised by the contents. Often there were many more cards than I expected. Sometimes fewer than I hoped. The sheer volume of the life I had lived overwhelmed me.

Could it be possible that I had the time in my years to fill each of these thousands or even millions of cards? But each card confirmed truth because they were all written in my handwriting and signed with my signature. When I pulled out the file marked "TV Shows I Have Watched," I realized the files grew to contain their contents. The cards were packed tightly, and yet after two or three yards, I hadn't found the end of the file. I shut it, shamed, not so much by the quality of shows but more by the vast time I knew that file represented.

When I came to a file marked "Lustful Thoughts," I felt a chill run through my body. I pulled the file out only an inch, not willing to test its size, and drew out a card. I shuddered at its detailed content. I felt sick to think such moments had been recorded. An almost animal rage broke on me. One thought dominated my mind: *"No one must ever see these cards! No one must ever see this room! I have to destroy them!"*

In insane frenzy, I yanked the file out. Its size didn't matter now. I had to empty it and burn the cards. But as I held it at one end and began pounding it on the floor, I could not dislodge a single card. I became desperate and pulled out a card, only to find it as strong as steel when I tried to tear it.

Defeated and utterly helpless, I returned the file to its slot. Leaning my forehead against the wall, I let out a long, self-pitying sigh. And then I saw it. The title bore "Times I've Spent Alone With God." The handle was brighter than those around it, newer, almost unused. I pulled on its handle, and a small box not more than three inches long fell into my hands. I could count on one hand the cards it contained. And then the tears came.

I began to weep with sobs so deep that they hurt. They started in my stomach and shook through me. I fell on my knees and cried from the overwhelming shame of it all. The rows of file shelves swirled in my tear-filled eyes. *No one must ever, ever know of this room. I must lock it up and hide the key.* But then, as I pushed away the tears, *I saw Him.*

No, please not Him. Not here. Oh, anyone but Jesus. I watched helplessly as He began to open the files and read the cards. I couldn't bear to watch His response. And in the moments when I could bring myself to look at His face, I saw a sorrow deeper than my own. He seemed intuitively to go to the worst boxes. Why did He have to read every one?

Finally, He turned and looked at me from across the room. He looked at me with pity in His eyes. But this was a pity that didn't anger me. I dropped my head, covered my face with my hands, and began to cry again. He walked over and put His arm around me. He could have said so many things, but He didn't say a word. He just cried with me.

Then He got up and walked back to the wall of files. Starting at one end of the room, He took out a file and, taking the cards one by one, began to sign His name over mine. "No!" I shouted, rushing to

Him. All I could find to say was "No, no," as I pulled the card from Him. His name shouldn't be on these cards. But there it was, written in red so rich, so dark, and so alive.

The name of Jesus covered mine. It was written with His blood. He gently took the card back. He smiled a sad smile and began to sign the cards. I don't think I'll ever understand how He did it so quickly, but seemingly in the next instant, I heard Him close the last file and walk back to my side. He placed His hand on my shoulder and said, "It is finished." I stood up, and He led me out of the room. There was no lock on the door. There are still more cards to be written.

We all have a room, don't we? We all have things we don't want others to know about, things we don't want them to see because if they did, they might not like us anymore. But here is the amazing thing—God has seen it all, and He still loves us. Can you imagine a friend who knew everything about you and still loved you? Now, that would be a true friend.

That's the God we have—a friend who wants a personal relationship with you. You can't hide your sins from Him. I want you to know that despite your sin, Jesus loves you. He wrote His name in blood across all your sins because they're already forgiven. Confess your sins, and He is faithful and just to forgive. You don't have to hide anything anymore!

FOR PERSONAL REFLECTION AND DISCUSSION

- What impacted you most about this story?
- How does this story make you want to change your life?

Chosen by God

The Bible tells us no one naturally seeks God on their own initiative, but God seeks them (Psalm 14:2). In John 1:43-51, Jesus called Philip to be His disciple. Philip, Andrew, and Peter lived in the same city. Philip then saw Nathanael and told him he had found the Messiah—Jesus of Nazareth, son of Joseph. Nathaniel remarked that nothing good comes out of Nazareth.

Jesus greeted him and said of him, "Behold, an Israelite in whom there is no conceit. Nathanael replied, "How do You know me?" Jesus answered, "Before Philip called you, when you were under the fig tree, I saw you." Nathanael had not met Him before and didn't know anything about Jesus when Philip approached him. Jesus knew Nathanael by name because he was chosen by God.

A young couple conceived a little boy when they were both students studying abroad. They were no longer together when the infant was born, and so the tiny one was placed for adoption. After one couple changed their minds about adopting the boy, another agreed. The new parents weren't well educated, and the adopting mother later admitted she was too frightened to love him for the first six months of his life, fearful that he might be taken from them.

By age two, the boy had become a difficult child, and the two felt they might have made a mistake and wanted to return him. As an adult, Steve Jobs would later say he was deeply loved and indulged by this couple and was upset when they were referred to as his "adoptive parents." He eventually became the co-founder and

CEO of Apple, and regarded them as his parents "1,000 percent."

If you have received Jesus Christ as your Savior, the Bible says you have been adopted by the Father (John 1:12). John 15:16 says, "You did not choose me, but I chose you." As a result of that adoption, as a full child of God, you are now entitled to the inheritance of a son of the Father (Colossians 1:12 and Ephesians 1:4-5). My youngest daughter is adopted, and I often tell her, "Your brothers and sisters had no choice in their parents, but we CHOSE you. Therefore you are special. You didn't inherit your parents; they chose you!"

Unlike Paul and Clara Jobs, even if you are a difficult child, God will never change His mind about you. He will keep you. He will never leave you or forsake you. He will sustain you until He brings you home to glory. His mind is made up about you!

Another non-biblical illustration is the classic S&H green stamps program, which was the first loyalty program ever developed. Stores would reward shoppers with green stamps based on their total purchase in their stores. My grandmother would never shop in a store that didn't give green stamps. She collected the stamps and glued them into books. When she had enough stamped books, she would redeem them for merchandise—lamps, toasters, chairs, vacuum cleaners, etc. There was a whole catalog of things that could be redeemed with these green stamps.

Today, we have all kinds of loyalty programs—airlines have frequent flyer miles that can be redeemed for free trips; hotels have frequent guest programs for free nights in their hotel; rental cars have loyalty programs; and even Mike's Subs has a loyalty program—if you buy ten subs then the eleventh sub is free.

But in earlier days, S&H green stamps were the trending thing. My grandmother would go to the redemption center and browse at all the merchandise to decide what she wanted. Finally, she would settle on something, redeem her green stamps for it, and proudly bring it home to show everyone.

Let's imagine that the human race is in a redemption center. God comes in looking around for people He wants to redeem. He wanders around and looks at many people. Everyone is hoping God picks them. Then one day God comes over and looks at me. I couldn't believe He was actually considering me. Then He walked up to the clerk in front and said, "I'd like to redeem that Steve White fellow." I could hear Him, and I was really excited.

The clerk said, "Oh Lord, you don't want him. He is one of our most expensive humans. He is handsome, smart, and very popular (ha-ha, the devil made me do it). You would need 100 books of green stamps for him." God says, "Green stamps? I don't have any green stamps." So the clerk asks God, "Well, what do you have?" And God says, "Well, I have my Son." The clerk then says to God, "Oh no, Lord, I couldn't let you do that. Your Son is worth a million times more than that Steve White guy." But God says, "Well, I think he is worth it."

Then God calls out my name to come forward, and I can't believe it. So I run to the front. God takes me by my right hand and tells me that I am now His, and He will always be with me. As we leave the redemption center, He turns back to clerk and says, "I'll be back; I have many more I want to redeem."

Now you might think that is just a cute story, but look at what God says in Isaiah 43:1-3,

> *Do not fear, for I have redeemed you; I have summoned you by name; and you are mine." Then God goes on to say, "When you pass through the waters, I will be with you; and when you pass through the rivers, they will not sweep over you. When you walk through the fire, you will not be burned; the flames will not set you ablaze. For I am the Lord your God, the Holy One of Israel, your Savior."*

Because I am forgiven, God has given me these promises! Now, that is pretty reassuring stuff!

When I think about God being with me when I pass through

the waters, I think of God parting the Red Sea for Moses as the children of Israel were fleeing Egypt (Exodus 14:19-29). Or I think of Joshua crossing the Jordan River with the Ark of the Covenant (Joshua 3:14-16).

And when I think of walking through the fire, I think of three Hebrew children—Shadrach, Meshach, and Abednego (Daniel 3:13-25). Those boys refused to bow down to the idol that King Nebuchadnezzar had built. So the king had them thrown into the fiery furnace. The furnace was so hot it killed the soldiers who put them in the furnace. When the king looked in the furnace, he saw four people, not just three, and they were walking around unbound and unharmed. As we know, the fourth person was Jesus Himself. When the king ordered the boys out of the furnace, they were not burned, their hair was not singed, their robes were not burned, and they didn't even smell like smoke. As a result, Nebuchadnezzar praised their God.

So God is ever with me—and with you, as a believer in Christ Jesus. God does forgive sins, no matter how bad you think they might be. Oh, the joy of hearing, "I do not condemn you." Knowing you are forgiven will make the biggest difference in your life!

FOR PERSONAL REFLECTION AND DISCUSSION

- How do you know you have been redeemed?
- Describe a tough time in your life when you knew God was with you.

5

Why God?

My high school baseball coach told me that as a pitcher, the most important thing was to pitch aggressively and get ahead in the count. I watch many Atlanta Braves games, and they have some outstanding, young pitchers. I hear the coaches and expert commentators tell them, even today, the exact same thing—pitch aggressively and get ahead in the count. It's just the most important thing to learn in pitching.

Joyce and I chose to write about God because He is the most important thing. We want people to know the truth about God—not what they think, heard, or feel about God, but what is actually true about God. We use the Bible as our baseline for that truth. Jesus said, "I am the way, the truth, and the life" (John 14:6). So right off the bat, we know that Truth is a person. And getting to know the truth is about getting to know a person. And when you know Jesus—you will know the Truth!

With that being said, we admit it is difficult to comprehend God. God is omnipotent (all-powerful), while most of the time, we feel powerless. God is omniscient (all-knowing), and yet the more we know, the more we realize how little we know. God is omnipresent (everywhere at once), and we have trouble staying in the moment. God is immutable (never changes), while we are constantly surrounded by change every day. No wonder we have difficulty comprehending the immensity of God.

But more than great, God is good. It's a fortunate thing a God this great is also good. What if a great and powerful God were not good? We could not survive. But God is love, full of grace, forgiving, patient, kind, generous, seeks only justice, is righteous and compassionate. He absolutely loves His creation.

Changing your mind can be transforming! In Romans 12:2, Paul tells us, "Do not be conformed to the pattern of this world, but be transformed by the renewing of your mind!" We need to be open to thinking differently about God. Just maybe what you've heard is not what was said, or what is true. Only the truth about Him will help us know Him better.

Paul has a lot to say about our thoughts and minds. In 2 Corinthians 10:5, he says to "take every thought captive and make it obedient to Christ." To the Philippians, he says, "Let this mind be in you which was also in Christ Jesus" (Philippians 2:5). In Romans 8:6, Paul says, "They have their minds set on the flesh (the world) which is death, but the mind set on the Spirit is life and peace!"

We choose to tell you about the God we know because nothing is more important than God. Our eternity depends on getting this right. Therefore, thinking rightly about God and knowing who He is becomes essential.

A Little History

Before we begin this adventure, we must say that God and the Bible are our change-enabling tools.

As a background, let's start with the creation. Genesis 1:1-2:2 gives the biblical account of the creation of the world in which we live. He created the first humans in His image (Gen 1:26-27); and to them alone, He gave a soul and the gift of free will.

His other creations lived by instinct, but He gave man alone the freedom to decide how he wanted to live and the ability to make his own decisions in everything. At the time of creation, man only knew good things. Likewise, God created woman as a helpmeet for the man, and she only knew good things (Genesis 2:18-25). They both were naked and unashamed in the Garden of Eden.

The first two created human beings—Adam and Eve—were enjoying life in the Garden of Eden. Then, in Genesis 3:1-7, using their gifts of free will, they made the wrong choice of eating the forbidden fruit. Eve succumbed to the serpent's temptation to eat the fruit and thereby know everything that God knows, and she persuaded Adam to eat the fruit as well. Because they disobeyed God's command not to eat the forbidden fruit, their eyes were opened, and they saw they were naked.

Each of them exercised his/her free will and got it wrong. The serpent used crafty persuasion in his temptation, and Eve rationalized it would be okay to eat the forbidden fruit. "When the woman saw that the tree was good for food and that it was a delight to the eyes, and that the tree was desirable to make one wise . . ." (Genesis 3:6). Thus, rationalization was introduced into the human mind, and the trap was set for all forthcoming human beings. Sin, in the form of disobedience to God's command, was born that day in the human heart.

We believe God is the ultimate Truth,. In Exodus 20:1-17, God gave Moses the Ten Commandments on Mount Sinai. (Today, many folks consider these commandments of God to be the Ten Suggestions, if they even consider them at all.)

When babies are born, psychologists say their minds are a *tabula rosa*—a clean slate with nothing written on it. As the children grow, they pick up beliefs from parents and siblings, from friends in the neighborhood, schoolmates, and things shown on the TV, etc. By the time the children become adults, both good and bad stuff have been written into their hearts and minds. So many of us carry these beliefs to the grave and never update or change them. (This concept of change is called transformation.)

In the following chapters, we want to share with you the God we know. We want you to know the truth about who He is, what He's like, how He operates, and what He thinks about you.

FOR PERSONAL REFLECTION AND DISCUSSION

- What attribute of God do you cherish most? Why?
- What makes God great to you?
- What makes God good to you?

6

Who Is God Anyway?

When my late son, David, was six years old, he gave his young heart to Jesus as his Savior and Lord in a heartfelt prayer. By that time, I was a divorced single parent and a somewhat new Christian myself, and David saw changes in my life as I began to grow in the Lord. I remember that night so many years ago—it was bedtime, and we were saying our evening prayers. I prayed Jesus would cover our house with His precious blood to protect us and everything He had given us to take care of on earth.

David was very sincere in his special request to be God's son by asking Jesus to be his heavenly Father. David was able to attend private Christian schools through elementary and high school, and we went to church on Sunday before he went to spend time with his earthly father. I was the custodial parent but encouraged his father to spend quality time with his son.

Everyone has a concept of who God is and whether or not He really exists. Everyone has been given a concept of good and evil, which is their morality gene when they were born. So why will this book, *The God I Know and the Relationship We Need,* do anything for anyone today or tomorrow? What's so special about God?

Imagine I am interviewing candidates for the position of "ruler of my life." I have interviewed quite a few from a large pool of candidates—wealth, health, substance addiction, sexuality, chaos, fear, doubt, anxiety, anger, hatred, mysticism, confusion, fame, power, etc. All the interviews began with an appealing promise of pleasure and security, but in the end, none of them were able to satisfy me.

Sigh! I have one final interview before I make a decision. My last interview is with God:

Me: Okay, God, thanks for showing interest in me and coming to this interview. I've heard a lot about You from other people, but I'm not sure you are relevant to me in these days. You see, I have received a lot of hearsay about You, and I want to talk about it. I also am not keen on giving anyone or anything complete control of my life.

God: Glad you invited Me to come to this interview. I would be pleased to hear about these ideas, and I would be happy to give you My take on them.

Me: One nagging thought on my mind says that I was an accident—my parents didn't want me, but they had me anyway. So how can I feel confident about myself? Why did You let this happen?

God: The Truth is I knew all about you when I created the earth in Genesis 1:1-2:2 (NASB). I chose your parents very carefully. I decided you would be born in this century, and I gave you many unique talents and gifts so you could grow up and do what only you were equipped to do. I gave you free will and an immortal soul and made you in Our image. You are unique and were not an accident, but a deliberate choice of Mine to be born!

Me: What do You mean in "Our image"?

God: I am a Spiritual Being, and I have three distinct entities in My Being. I am God the Father, Creator of the Universe—the heavens and earth and land and sea and all living creatures. I am God the Son, Jesus Christ, the Messiah who loved you so much I left My heavenly throne to be born as a baby and grow up to be an ultimate sacrifice for sin. I preached the Good News, performed miracles, and died on a cross to save you from the punishment of your sins and provided salvation by My atonement. And I am the Holy Spirit, advocate and counselor and teacher that resides in your soul and walks with you daily through every part of your day.

Me: My goodness, that's an incredibly busy workload You have! How would You have the time to be the Lord of my life? I need a lot of supervision! I need a lot of compassion and love, and I guess I need a lot of forgiveness and mercy as well. That makes me high maintenance.

God: I am God, your heavenly Father, and am not limited by time or space or gravity. I can do everything at the same time and not lose track of anything or anybody. I see all things, I am all-powerful, I am all-knowing, I am everywhere at once, and I never change!

- I am Light, pure and eternal light (1 John 1:5-7 NASB) and in Me is no darkness at all.
- I am Love, perfect and holy love for all that I have created. (1 John 4:8, 16 NASB)
- I am Holy, worthy of all praise and worship! (Revelation 4:8 NASB)
- I am Just, and I have prepared all things for you that eyes have not seen and ears have not heard for those who love Me (1 Corinthians 2:9 NASB).
- I am Righteous, and My throne is eternal (Hebrews 1:8 NASB).
- I am Peace, and I am not a God of chaos (1 Corinthians 14:33 NASB).
- I am Joy that comes with righteousness and peace (Romans 14:17 NASB).
- I am Suffering, and I sent My only Son, Jesus Christ, who as a man, endured sorrows and was acquainted with grief, was despised and not esteemed by men, and carried your sorrows and sins to the Cross (Isaiah 53:1-12 NASB).
- I am Mercy to all who call to Me (2 Corinthians 1:3 NASB).
- I am Healing of body, mind, and spirit for My children (Luke 9:11 NASB).
- I am the Father of all mankind (Luke 10:22 NASB).

Me: Whoa! I never knew all that! And You say that as my Father in heaven, You have a unique plan for my life, not for calamity but for a future and a hope?

God: That's absolutely right! You are My child and My own unique creation, and I love you!

Me: How do I know I can trust You with my life?

God: Look around you and see My other children. Read the Bible about the Old Testament Fathers of the faith, sinners who became saints, prophets in the Bible who spoke My words to kings and others. My guaranteed promise is that I will never leave you or forsake you or give up on you! And you can take that to the bank!

Me: Wow, I think I might sign You up as the ruler of my life! What do I have to do to get this perfect life plan?

God: Ask My Son, Jesus Christ, to be the Lord and Savior of your life—confess you are a sinner and that you surrender your life to me as God and let Me lead you in the purpose for your life!

Me: Sounds a bit scary to give You complete control, God! That's a lot to take in. Let me get back to You on this! Maybe I can give You a couple of rooms in my life to live in on a trial basis.

God: Okay, I can wait, but I like what I see, and so does Jesus!

Be assured you will not see this interview on CNN, MSNBC, or social media because they deny God before men. The power of Christ in me will keep me safely in God's mighty hand and His holy will until Christ returns or You take me home, Father God! On the basis of these new facts about God's love, compassion, and mercy that you just learned, search your own heart about who you think God is and your concept of Him. Then ask the Lord to give you the grace to accept Him as your Savior and Lord. You will never regret it!

FOR PERSONAL REFLECTION AND DISCUSSION

- What would you ask God if you could interview Him?
- What makes God most real to you?

7

Oh, the Miracles

In the early 1960s, President John F. Kennedy told the American people that we would put a man on the moon (and bring him home safely) by the end of the decade. While it was a great vision, it seemed to me like an impossible thing. How could they possibly do it? There was just too much science and technology to figure out. We would need to develop propulsion systems, re-entry heat shields, oxygen, cabin pressurization, and an enormous list of other things I'm sure I couldn't even imagine.

No wonder that when we actually did it, there were conspiracy theories that the whole thing had been filmed and choreographed in Arizona. It was just too hard for some people to believe that landing a man on the moon was true.

I'm not surprised at all when people say they cannot believe all the miraculous things recorded in the Bible. These people conclude biblical miracles must be figurative and not literal because it boggles their mind to believe them to be true. For example, they take one passage of the Bible and say it is unbelievable and impossible, like the story of Jonah. "C'mon, Jonah and the whale? That story can't be taken literally. You can't be serious!"

My answer always remains the same:"Why not? Just because you can't explain it, doesn't mean it isn't true." It's no different than putting a man on the moon. The Bible is filled with incredible, literal occurrences and miracles. Take a look at a few of them:

- God speaks matter into existence (Genesis 1:31)
- Noah and the flood (Genesis 6:8–9:29)
- Parting the Red Sea for Moses (Exodus 13:17–14:31)
- Manna from heaven (Numbers 11:6-9)
- Samson pushing apart pillars (Judges 16:13-31)
- Hebrew children in a fiery furnace (Daniel 3:8-30)
- Jonah and the whale (Jonah 1:1–2:10)
- Virgin birth (Luke 1:24-37, 2:1-7)
- Resurrection from the dead (John 19:17-30; 20:1-17)

Jesus and some of His disciples also performed many miracles that were equally incredible:

- Turning water into wine (John 2:1-10)
- Making blind people see (Luke 18:35-43), (Mark 8:22-26), (John 9:1-7)
- Making lame people walk (Acts 3:2-8), (Acts 14:8-10)
- Cleansing lepers (Mark 1:40-45), (Luke 17:11-19)
- Raising people from the dead (Mark 5:21-24, 35-42), (John 11:1-44)
- Walking on water (Matthew 14:22-33)
- Feeding 5,000 people with a couple of fish and loaves of bread (Matthew 14:15-21)
- Calming the wind and the waves at sea (Luke 8:22-25)

The human mind can't explain *any* of these things, just like I can't explain how we put a man on the moon. But can we believe they are true? Some people go through these lists of miracles and choose the ones that make the most sense and tend to disbelieve the others. But, in truth, they view all miracles as figurative, not literal, because they can't explain any of them. I believe that we need to either accept them all or reject them all.

Indeed, the Bible is either all true, or none of it is true!

I have relatives who refuse to believe some of the things in the Bible. Jonah living in the belly of the whale for three days is just not believable to them. Yet, these same relatives have no trouble believing in the virgin birth or Christ's resurrection from the dead. Now I ask you, which is harder to believe—surviving three days in a whale or being raised from the dead? Both of these two events are mind-boggling! It just doesn't make any sense to me to believe one and not the other.

One day Jesus was teaching, and the Pharisees were in attendance. Some men came carrying a paralyzed man on a mat to see Jesus. The crowd was too large to get through, so they went up on the roof, removed some tiles, and lowered him to be in front of Jesus. When Jesus saw their faith, He told the paralyzed man his sins were forgiven.

The Pharisees went berserk and accused Jesus of blasphemy. Jesus knew their thoughts and said, "Which is easier to say, 'Your sins are forgiven' or to say, 'Get up and walk'?" Jesus then told the paralyzed man to get up, take his mat, and go home. And he did! Which do you think was easier for the Pharisees to believe? Anybody that could make a paralyzed man walk was probably also able to forgive sins. If you can believe one miracle, you can believe them all.

Do you know if you go through the Bible and choose the parts you believe and the parts you don't believe, then it is no longer the Bible—it is now the Gospel according to you! The Bible says all scripture is useful for teaching, rebuking, correcting, and training in righteousness (2 Timothy 3:16). God inspired all of its 66 books in their entirety. You can't add anything or take anything away, otherwise, the Bible becomes *your* word and not *His* word.

In Matthew 5:17-18, Jesus says He did not come to abolish

the Law and the Prophets (the cornerstone of the Jewish faith, the Old Testament), but to fulfill them. Until heaven and earth pass away, not one letter or stroke of the pen will pass away from His Word, the Bible.

The Bible says if all the things were written that could be written, the whole world couldn't contain it all (John 21:25). This statement means the Bible is just the studying points—the *Cliff Notes*. It's like God said, "This is what you really need to know now. This is the stuff that is really important. Get this part right, and everything else will be made clear one day."

I accept God's Word (Bible) totally on faith. I don't understand it all; I can't explain it all, but I believe it all. Everything I know about God teaches me to trust Him for all those things that I don't know or understand. It's called faith.

The miracle I personally cherish the most is that He saved a sinner like me, and part of that miracle is that He knows my name. He is the same God who created heaven and earth, spoke matter into existence, and breathed life into a human being—and He knows my name!

Whether you believe the miracles in the Bible or not; whether you can explain them or not—the true message of the Bible is this:

- God loves you.
- You are a sinner.
- The punishment for your sin is death.
- Christ's death on the cross paid the penalty for *your* sins.
- Salvation and forgiveness are gifts to you from God.
- For God so loved the world that He gave His only Son, that whoever believes in Him will not perish but have everlasting life (John 3:16).

I want you to know you can trust God. And maybe it's time for you to have faith and accept the Bible as literally true. You can have faith and trust the Bible is true, whether you can explain it or not!

And you can take that to the bank!

FOR PERSONAL REFLECTION AND DISCUSSION

- What miracle is hardest for you to believe? Why?
- What miracle of Jesus do you cherish most? Why?
- When Peter walked on water, why do you think he started to sink? Does your answer apply to you?

8

The Love Letter

I remember when my wife and I were dating, occasionally I would get a card or letter from her saying she missed me, or she loved me and couldn't wait to be together with me again. Those were some of the most uplifting moments for me. To know that she loved me and wanted to be with me just meant everything to me.

I cherished those love letters. Sometimes it was just a phone call or a quick message that always put a smile on my face. And I know she cherished the times I sent her a note or gave her a call. Knowing somebody loves you is just the greatest comfort. It warms your heart.

That is the way I view the Bible. I believe the Bible is a love letter from home—from our heavenly Father. Paul stated that our citizenship is in heaven; he saw himself as an alien on earth as an ambassador for Christ. Paul boldly proclaimed the Gospel message because he wanted people to know Christ died for their sins and that believing in Him would lead them to eternal life. Paul wanted people to know Christ and the power of His resurrection in their hearts. If I could sum up the entire Bible in three words, they would be "God loves you!"

Have you ever met someone who viewed the Bible as a rule book, beating you up with it whenever you did something they thought was wrong? Aren't they miserable people? Their self-righteousness would be enough to discourage anyone from searching for God and His salvation! It certainly turns me off!

The Bible contains 66 books, the bulk of which—the Old

Testament—was written before the birth of Jesus Christ. These books include God's commandments as well as religious laws to define and govern ancient Israel. The Old Testament also records the history of the Jewish people and contains psalms, proverbs, and prophecies.

The New Testament records the birth, adult life, and the death and resurrection of Jesus Christ. He not only fulfills the law and the prophecies about Himself, He expands the Ten Commandments in the New Testament, which became the foundation of the Christian faith! The remainder of the New Testament includes the teachings of Paul and others, ending with the Book of Revelation.

It seems like some Christians feel they need to forcibly implant the word of God into your mind for your good. I have a friend who uses his Bible as a weapon to confront people about their sins and challenges them to change their way of life to be more pleasing to God. I believe this person is a Christian who loves the Lord, but I also know he has offended more people than he has led to the Lord. He loves God, but instead of sharing God's love, he shares a rule book.

God gave the Jews the Ten Commandments to show them how He expected them to live. But they also showed how futile it would be to think you could possibly keep them all. Can anyone honestly say they've kept all the commandments? No one! So why verbally beat someone up with a set of rules you yourself can't keep? That's hypocritical.

The Bible certainly contains some rules and commandments for how God wants us to live our lives, but I don't view them as a rule book. I view them as God's guidelines for successful living, not to restrict me, but to show me the land mines I need to avoid. These guidelines are from God's heart of love.

The Bible's theme is not rules but fellowship with Him and His love! It's as if God said, "You can't understand everything yet, so just get this part right—I love you!" God sent His only Son to die as an atonement for our sins! What greater love is there than this?

Don't get me wrong; the Bible has much to say about righteous living. As Christians, we should read the entire Bible for ourselves and trust the Holy Spirit to guide us toward Christ-likeness. But, while righteous living is a good thing, it is not the focus of the Bible. The focus of the Bible is to tell us Jesus is the Savior of the world, and His redeeming power reconciles sinful man to Himself. Christ gave us a great example to follow, and we should strive to emulate Him.

As Stephen Covey would say, "The main thing, is to keep the main thing, the main thing." And the main thing I want you to know is that God loves you unconditionally and sent Jesus to die for your sins so you could have fellowship with Him forever!

The Bible is the greatest love letter ever written. Read the Gospel of John in your Bible as a love letter from God personally to you. And the truth of God's love will set you free!

FOR PERSONAL REFLECTION AND DISCUSSION

- How well do you think you love your neighbor as yourself? How can you improve?
- How do God's laws and love come together for you?
- In 25 words or less, what do you think is the message of the Bible?

9

Important to God

I heard a story about a man and his wife who recently moved into a new neighborhood. It must be an older story because it describes people hanging their clothes outside on a clothesline to dry after they were washed. One morning, he and his wife were having coffee at the breakfast table, which was in front of a window. The wife saw the next-door neighbor hanging out her laundry and remarked to her husband how dirty the clothes looked. The husband smiled and said nothing.

Over the next several weeks, the wife would make the same remark to him every time she saw her neighbor hanging out the laundry. One day the husband washed their kitchen window, unbeknownst to his wife. The next morning, as they were having their usual morning coffee, the wife noted how much cleaner her neighbor's laundry looked than before. She remarked to her husband, "She must be using a new laundry detergent!"

We Americans love to see stereotypes of personalities in the movies and on TV shows and the nightly news, etc. You may see someone who epitomizes a particular personality like a drama queen, a braggart, a macho man, or a fire-breathing politician. Some movies feature gang wars in the inner cities of America, where a gang leader or member would respond to a question by saying, "Are you talkin' to me?"

Other movie actors might ask, "Are you somebody important?" Seemingly, these types of behaviors reflect a superiority complex, by which people think of themselves as being more important, more famous, or a better person than others. In their eyes, others are beneath them in the pecking order of life. Why should they take a moment of their time and respond to a question unless they can put others down with their answers? After all, it's all about them!

Our arrogance and self-righteous opinions do not draw people into friendship because no one likes to be put down. That also goes for gossiping, self-comparison, and comments based on our race, financial status, country of origin, etc. If we feel we are better than others, we make them feel unworthy to be with us.

This also goes for how we feel about other people who go to our church or Bible study. We enjoy our status in comfortable pews, looking down on others who we consider to be unacceptable. Perhaps they are struggling through a divorce or a serious illness in the family, wear hand-me-down clothes because their budgets are too tight to afford new clothes, or have a car that could qualify to be an antique.

There is no evidence of arrogance with God, and He never treats His creation that way! That very attitude of pride and arrogance was the downfall of Lucifer, a former angel of light, when he dared to try to dethrone God.

Luke 10:16-18 (NASB) tells the story of the seventy disciples, sent out by twos, to preach the Good News of the Kingdom of God everywhere they went. Jesus said to them before they left, "The one who listens to you listens to me, and the one who rejects you rejects Me; and he who rejects Me rejects the One Who sent me (God the Father)." When the seventy disciples returned, they marveled, saying, "Even the demons are subject to us in Your name." Jesus replied, "I was watching Satan fall from heaven like lightning!"

The devil is a sore loser! The devil will use whatever he can to cause division and keep you from the truth. In 1 Peter 5:6-8 (NASB), Peter tells us to

Therefore humble yourself under the mighty hand of God, that He might exalt you at the proper time, casting all your

anxiety on Him because He cares for you. Be of sober spirit, be on the alert. Your adversary, the devil, prowls around like a roaring lion, seeking someone to devour.

His mantra is that if he can't have you, no one—even God—can have you!

The devil is a diabolical stalker and thief whose sole purpose is to fan the flames of your pride, arrogance, and holier-than-thou attitude and keep you from accepting the free gift of salvation. He was forever defeated at the cross of Calvary and humiliated at the resurrection of Jesus from the dead. He will never get over the fact that his eternal fate was sealed by the blood of Jesus!

The Book of Proverbs shares some golden nuggets of truth regarding pride. Proverbs 16:18 (NASB) says that pride goes before destruction, and a haughty spirit before stumbling. Proverbs 21:4 (NASB) tells us that "haughty eyes and a proud heart, the lamp of the wicked, is sin." But the Good News is that Jesus bids all who are weary and heavy laden to come to Him, and He will give them rest.

Take My yoke upon you and learn from Me, for I am gentle and humble in heart and you will find rest for your souls for My yoke is easy and My burden is light (Matthew 11:28-30 NASB).

Paul writes,

Through the grace that was given to me, I say to all among you not to think more highly of himself than he ought to think; but to think so as to have sound judgment, as God has allotted to each of measure of faith (Romans 12:3 NASB).

Further in the chapter, Paul says that we should

Be of the same mind toward one another, do not be haughty in mind, but associate with the lowly. Do not be wise in your own estimation (Romans 12:16 NASB).

Finally, Paul remarks that if anyone thinks he is something when he is nothing, he deceives himself (Galatians 6:3 NASB). That's a shocker to the proud and arrogant person! Jesus said,

> *How can you say to your brother, "Brother let me take the speck out of your eye" when you yourself fail to see the plank in your own eye? You hypocrite, first take the plank out of your own eye, and then you will see clearly to remove the speck from your brother's eye* (Luke 6:42 NASB).

God is love, and His love embraces humility and servanthood to others by His definition, "Love thy neighbor as thyself"! Yes, God wants you to become somebody important—make Jesus your Lord and Savior, love your neighbor as yourself, and change the world!

FOR PERSONAL REFLECTION AND DISCUSSION

- Do you sometimes think you are better than others? Why, why not?
- How do you overcome the tendency to do that?
- What does servanthood mean to you? What makes you good at it?

10

He Wants To Help

I remember when my kids were tiny, they were completely dependent on my wife and me for virtually everything. As they grew, they learned to do more and more on their own. We used to measure their growth by how lighter the diaper bag was getting. When they gave up bottles and formula, the diaper bag wasn't so heavy anymore. When they got to be around two years old, they thought they were ready to dress themselves—but they weren't.

When I would say, "Let me help you with that," quickly they would reply, "I can do it myself." After a time of frustration, they would come reluctantly and ask for help. We're the same way with God. We don't want His help until we get frustrated and give up!

We live in a world today that glorifies self. We love self-made people, we admire people with great self-worth, and we applaud people with self-confidence. And there are many more "self" attributes that we glorify, such as: self-assured, self-control, self-conscious, and self-esteem. We often think we are indestructible like Superman or Mighty Mouse. Our motto is "I got this," even when we are falling off a cliff!

"Real men and real women don't need any outside help" is a popular mantra in today's world. Faith is for those people who cannot face reality. How can I trust somebody that I can't see to come down from heaven and help me? After all, this is my life and my kingdom of self; I am self-sufficient, and I don't need or want any help!

However, the Bible isn't so big on self-glorification. In

Romans 2:8, Paul says, "Those who are self-seeking and who reject the truth and follow evil, there will be wrath and anger."
Focusing on self detracts from focusing on God. Further, in
Romans 6:6, Paul says, "For we know that our old self was crucified with him [Jesus]." The Bible teaches that when Christ died, we
died too. Our new resurrected life is to be His life. It is no longer a
matter of self-effort but rather Jesus living His life through us. You
cannot save yourself by your own efforts!

Self-focus also keeps us from calling on God for help. Most
people cry out to God for help with the really big things. But most
people tend not to ask God for help with something they know they
can do themselves. They don't want to bother God with things they
think they can handle. But God wants to be involved in everything
we do, even trivial things.

God wants to help us find something we have misplaced or a
parking space at the crowded mall. He is always available! He
longs to be with you, and He wants you to have faith in Him 24/7.
He longs to converse with you all day long.

God is not impressed with "self." In fact, God says all our self-
righteousness is as filthy rags to Him. God is deeply impressed
with His Son, and we inherit Jesus' righteousness when we accept
Christ as our Lord and Savior. We achieve salvation through faith,
which is also a gift from God. Paul said, "For it is by grace that you
are saved through faith" (Ephesians 2:8). It is by God's grace we
receive salvation simply by faith.

The Bible has so much to say about faith. Read Hebrews 11
and learn about the hall of faith. Many men and women in the
Bible displayed great faith in their lives—Abraham, Noah, and
Daniel, just to name a few. Hebrews 11:6 says,

*Without faith it is impossible to please God, because
anyone who comes to him must believe that He exists and
that He rewards those who earnestly seek Him.*

Faith is defined as, "Confidence in what we hope for and assurance about what we do not see." Just saying, "Oh well, I certainly hope so" is not expressing a confident hope. Most of us have assurance about the things we can see. And we even have assurance about some things we don't see—like our car will start, and we'll get a dial-tone when we pick up the phone. But do we have that same assurance about God?

The Bible also says faith without works is dead (James 2:17). James, the Lord's brother, tells us not to be just hearers of the Word but to also be doers of the Word. Christians usually show their faith by their deeds. It does no good to see someone without clothes or food and tell them to keep warm and well-fed. Faith in action will feed and clothe that person. It is not a matter of just knowing what to do—it is also a matter of doing it! Faith demonstrated in action is the idea.

Many people have asked me about the difference between faith, belief, and trust. Webster's dictionary defines them this way:

- **Faith**—complete confidence in something or someone; loyalty or allegiance to a cause or person
- **Belief**—to accept as true; be confident about something; firm conviction about the goodness of something or someone
- **Trust**—complete confidence in a person or plan; certainty based on past experience; the trait of believing in the honesty and reliability in someone

Imagine yourself standing on one side of the Grand Canyon, and there is a rope connecting your side to the other side. Belief is seeing the rope, faith believes the rope will hold you, and trust is walking on the rope to the other side. Trust is when you reach the end of the light you have, and God tells you to take one more step. If you obey and take one more step, then you can be sure of one of two things—God is going to put something underneath your feet, or He's going to teach you to fly!

As I write this today, my health is poor. I have renal cell carcinoma, B-cell non-Hodgkin's Lymphoma, and stage 5 chronic kidney disease (CKD). I was on the transplant list for a new kidney at Emory University Hospital, but I'm no longer eligible because of my cancer. But my faith in God is stronger than ever. I have no fear, no anxiety, and great peace about my situation.

God created me, and I know He loves me. I trust Him with my life. And it is my absolute total trust in Him that brings such peace—the peace that surpasses all understanding. If I am to continue to live, God will make a way, and I will make sure He gets all the glory. And if I am to die soon, I know that my citizenship is in heaven, and I will be seeing Him face to face very soon, and that is certainly not a bad thing. The Apostle Paul said, "To live is Christ, and to die is gain" (Philippians 1:21).

So, what about you? Where is your citizenship? One day, you're going to die just like me. None of us get out of this world alive, you know. Salvation is only one small step of faith away. Will you take that step? God loves you and sent His Son to die on a cross to take the punishment for your sins. Believe that truth in your heart, and your newfound faith in Him will guarantee you eternal life. I hope I'll be seeing you there!

God doesn't want you to live a solitary life. He wants to live life with you—actively. The idea is laboring with Him—not for Him. He wants to come along beside you, share your life with you, converse with you, and laugh and cry with you. Don't be self-sufficient another day. Don't tell God, "I can do it myself." You can do all things through Christ Jesus, who strengthens me!

FOR PERSONAL REFLECTION AND DISCUSSION

- What is the difference between faith, belief, and trust to you?
- Describe a time when you should have invited God to help you.
- Describe a time when you exhibited great faith in God.

11

The WOW of Forgiveness

I have a friend who recently lost his youngest son. I don't know all the circumstances of the boy's death, but I know the father was devastated. He kept looking back at things he could have done that might have made a difference and saved his son. He was beating himself up and believing that God could never forgive him for not having done something that might have saved his child.

And I know there are many people like my friend. And many, at least, believe in God, so that is a good start. But my question to them is always the same, "What if He could forgive your sin? Would that make any difference for you?"

Can you imagine what a difference that would make in a person's life? Imagine life for someone who believed God could never forgive them. They would always believe they were condemned. How would that make them feel—probably miserably resigned to their fate?

But, if they could see themselves as forgiven, would that make a difference in their lives? Yes, of course, it would. That new belief—the difference between "I'm condemned" versus "I'm forgiven"—would change how they feel about everything! Their behavior would change dramatically, and the results they'd create for themselves would be totally different. Would that better meet their needs? It sure would, no doubt about it.

So, if you think your sin is beyond God's forgiveness, then this chapter is for you! The first thing you need to know is ALL have sinned and fallen short of the glory of God (Romans 3:23). So you're not alone as a sinner. The Bible also says the wages of sin is death (Romans 6:23). So the penalty of sin for all of us is death. The Bible also says that without the shedding of blood, there can be no forgiveness of sin (Hebrews 9:22). So there can be forgiveness for sin, but it *must* involve the shedding of blood.

In Old Testament days, the Jews sacrificed animals on the altar so their sins could be forgiven. They had to do so because of their ongoing sins. But that changed when Jesus became the ultimate sacrifice. The Bible tells us that the shedding of Christ's blood is what forgives our sin. Hebrews 9:12 tells us this,

> He [Jesus] *did not enter by means of the blood of goats and calves; but He entered the Most Holy Place once for all by His own blood, thus obtaining eternal redemption* [forgiveness].

It was Jesus' blood sacrifice and death that ensures our forgiveness. And it was for all—dying once for all. He needs no more sacrifice because His Son paid it all. God gives us this gift of forgiveness when we accept Jesus as our Savior and Lord.

The only thing remaining for us to do is to confess our sins to God. The Bible says, "If we confess our sins, He is faithful and just and will forgive us our sins and purify us from all unrighteousness" (1 John 1:9). God is not only faithful, but He is also just. He is justified in forgiving our sins because Jesus has paid the debt of all of our sins already. So when Satan accuses us of sin, it's as if God says, "I'm sorry, Satan, but that debt has already been paid."

Perhaps a bigger challenge for you is that once you can see God has forgiven you, can you forgive yourself? You cannot continue to see yourself as unforgivable if God sees you as already forgiven. If you struggle with this, I would advise seeking the assistance of a good Christian counselor. These people are trained to help people work through this issue. You are not alone!

There are also many examples of biblical characters who sinned greatly, and God forgave them. The first would be King

David himself. David was a murderer and an adulterer. In 2 Samuel 11:1-27, David saw Bathsheba, wife of Uriah, bathing on a rooftop, he desired to sleep with her, and she conceived a child. David later arranged to place Uriah, a valiant soldier, in the midst of a great battle so that he would be killed in order for David to marry Bathsheba. Yet God forgave him.

David repented and turned to the Lord with a broken and contrite heart. And David was so sincere in his repentance that later God said David was a man after His own heart. And God promised to bring forth His Son Jesus Christ through David's lineage.

And then there was Simon Peter, one of Jesus' twelve disciples, the impetuous one who cut off a soldier's ear when they came to arrest Jesus. He's the one who promised Jesus he would never leave him on the night Jesus was arrested. Then Peter denied Jesus, even swore he never knew Him three times (Luke 22:54-62). Can you imagine his shame when the rooster crowed, and Peter remembered that Jesus had foretold Peter's denial? He wept bitterly.

And yet Peter went on to become the lead apostle, proclaiming the Gospel on the morning of Pentecost when 3000 people gave their lives to Jesus. Peter went on to write two books bearing his name in the New Testament and became the rock upon which Jesus said He would build His church and the gates of hell would not prevail against it.

And then there was the Jewish woman taken in adultery (John 6:3-11). The Pharisees had brought her to Jesus, trying to trap him and accuse him of violating Jewish law. Jesus quietly said to the crowd, "Let him who is without sin cast the first stone." The accusers all knew they were sinners too, and the crowd soon began to disperse. Soon it was just Jesus and the adulteress.

Jesus said to her, "Woman, where are they? Has no one condemned you?" She replied, "No one, Sir." Jesus then tells her, "Then neither do I condemn you. Go now and leave your life of sin." Can you imagine her relief? Her belief changed in an instant—from "I'm an adulteress" to "I am forgiven." Do you think that changed the way she felt? Do you think it changed her behavior? Do you think she began creating new results in her life that better met her needs? Do you think her testimony (story) of how Jesus forgave her sin made a big impression on the Jewish people?

If God can forgive David, Peter, and the adulteress, don't you think He can forgive you? You are precious in His sight. Like the Prodigal Son, when you repent and come home, God has compassion. He will run to greet you, He will hug you, and His whole Kingdom will become yours. And He will celebrate with you!

Close your eyes for one second, and imagine Jesus standing in front of you. He says to you what He said to the adulteress, "I do not condemn you," and then He hugs you. That, my friend, is a WOW moment.

And this is possible because Jesus, God's only Son, died on the cross for your sins. Your debt has been paid. You are free from guilt and shame because you have been redeemed by the blood of the spotless Lamb of God! In Psalm 103:12, God says He has removed our sins from us as far as the East is from the West. In Isaiah 43:25, God says He will remember our sins no more. And that's good enough for me.

In Psalm 130:3-4, the writer says, "If you, Lord, kept a record of sins, who could stand? But with you, Lord, there is forgiveness." If God kept a list of every one of our sins, then none of us would have a chance. But God is a forgiving God, and He wants all people to come to repentance and receive forgiveness.

In Acts 10:43, Luke tells us that, "All the prophets testify about Him (Jesus) that everyone who believes in Him receives forgiveness of sins through His name." Our sins are forgiven because we believed in Jesus and accepted Him as our Savior. Paul says, "For it is by grace that we are saved through faith—and this is not from yourselves, it is a gift of God—not by works, so that no one can boast (Ephesians 2:8). The Apostle Paul preached, "Therefore, my friends, I want you to know that through Jesus the forgiveness of sins is proclaimed to you (Acts 13:38).

I want you to know that when you know in your heart that God has forgiven you—there is no better feeling in the world. The weight of the world is lifted off your shoulders, and you'll just say, "WOW!"

FOR PERSONAL REFLECTION AND DISCUSSION

- How do you overcome your guilt? How do you help others?
- Why is forgiving yourself so hard?
- Is there a sin that cannot be forgiven? Explain.

12

That Older Brother

Maybe you're familiar with siblings and their rivalries—they compete for everything. And they're often jealous when one gets attention, and the other doesn't. I just have one brother who is nine years younger. We didn't have much rivalry at all because of our age difference. But I have a couple of granddaughters who wrote the book on rivalry. They are two years apart and have competed in everything, most notably in tennis.

They were both very good tennis players, but the younger one got to be a little better, and there was definitely some jealousy. As they've aged, the competitiveness has given way to a true friendship. Unfortunately, the same thing can't be said about the Prodigal Son and his older brother.

You remember in the first chapter, we talked about the prodigal son. The saddest story in the Bible to me is the prodigal's older brother. Understandably, he feels neglected and unappreciated. After all, he was loyal to his father. The sad part is "why" he felt that way.

"Meanwhile, the older son was in the field. When he came near the house, he heard music and dancing. So he called one of the servants and asked him what was going on. 'Your brother has come,' he replied, 'and your father has killed the fattened calf because he has him back safe and sound.'

"The older brother became angry and refused to go in.

49

So his father went out and pleaded with him. But he answered his father, 'Look! All these years I've been slaving for you and never disobeyed your orders. Yet you never gave me even a young goat so I could celebrate with my friends. But when this son of yours who has squandered your property with prostitutes comes home, you kill the fattened calf for him!'

"'My son,' the father said, 'you are always with me, and everything I have is yours. But we had to celebrate and be glad, because this brother of yours was dead and is alive again; he was lost and is found'" (Luke 15:25-32).

So the older son wanted to know what all the commotion was about and asked one of the servants. The servant told him his brother was home, and his father was celebrating his return. The older brother became angry and refused to join the party. He clearly thought, *My brother doesn't deserve this; he is the one who left home. He should be punished.*

But look who takes the initiative—the father. The father left the party and went out and pleaded with the older son to join the celebration. What a loving father! He clearly wanted to celebrate with both his sons. The father didn't wait in the house; he went out to the older son. In the same way, God approaches us when we are angry and stubborn and believe something false.

The older son then proceeded to tell his father all the things he felt. "I've been loyal all these years and never disobeyed you. You've never given me anything to celebrate with my friends. This son squandered your money with prostitutes, and now you kill the fattened calf for him?" So having these feelings, what did the older brother do? He chose not to attend the celebration. And as a result of that action, he missed the joyous celebration.

After venting his anger and frustration to his father, the father responded, "Son, you are always with me, and all that I have is yours." And this is the saddest thing in the Bible to me—the older son had *everything* and didn't know it. Every child of God has everything! That's you, and that's me! We have it all! What a shame not to know it. And further, it shows the older son didn't even know his own father and the love and compassion and caring he had for both his two sons.

And then, the father said, "We had to celebrate and be glad. This brother of yours was dead and is alive again. He was lost and is now found." The operative words here are "had to celebrate." It is not an option for God. His love for His children demands celebration when they are found and come home. This is not a choice for God—it is an auto-response. This is just who He is and what His love for you demands of Himself.

Although it is not recorded in the Bible, I like to think the older brother had an epiphany after his Father spoke to him. He just might have come to believe, "My Father loves me and all that he has is mine." I like to think he then joined the celebration to honor his younger brother's return home.

We have a loving heavenly Father, who is compassionate, who will run to you, hug you, and celebrate with you and for you. Regardless of what you may believe or may have heard, the truth is you have a heavenly Father who loves you that much. Isn't it time you came home?

FOR PERSONAL REFLECTION AND DISCUSSION

- Why do you think the father went out to talk to the older son?
- When talking to the older son, why do you think the father said they *had* to celebrate?
- Why do you think so many Christians today are like the older son?

13

The *Cliff Notes*

When my granddaughter was about four years old, she was having a discussion with my wife, who she calls "Bama" (that's just the way "Grandma" first came out of her mouth, and every grandchild since then calls her Bama). Maybe three minutes into a story Bama was telling her, my four-year-old granddaughter says, "Just give me the bottom line, Bama," She didn't want the whole story; she just wanted the bottom line. And some people feel that way about the Bible—just give me the bottom line.

And the Bible is sometimes hard to understand—it's big and bulky; it comes in so many different versions and has weird language and unpronounceable names in it. And some people say, "So that's why I never read it. It makes no sense to me. There aren't even any pictures—only page after page of small black print until you get to the end parts, and then there are some in red print. So why should I waste any of my time trying to read it?"

All of these statements tend to be true to someone who has never seen a Bible, let alone read it. But the Bible is the written word of God, His Truth. So, this chapter is the *Cliff Notes* (a small book that contains the gist of a book without having to read the whole thing). It's kind of a cheat sheet so you can get a quick idea of what is in the Bible, how it is arranged, and what is the theme or overall message of the Bible. (Hopefully, you will want to read the whole Bible on your own someday.)

The Bible contains 66 little books within a single book. Its main division is between the Old Testament and the New

Testament. The Bible begins with the Old Testament statement, "In the beginning, God created the heavens and the earth" (Genesis 1:1) and proceeds to record God's creation of the earth. In Genesis, you hear about Adam and Eve, Cain and Abel, Noah, Abraham, and Moses.

The next book, Exodus, tells how God led Moses and His people out of Egypt into the Promised Land and the giving of the Ten Commandments to Moses. The next three books—Leviticus, Numbers, and Deuteronomy—give census figures and describe Jewish law that had to be observed by the Israelites. These five books are called the Torah—the basis of Jewish law. Then you have chapters that record the history of the Israelites until the time of Jesus.

There are also non-history books—Psalms (a songbook), Proverbs (nuggets of wisdom), and the prophetic books from Isaiah to Ezekiel to Jeremiah to a long list of Minor Prophets. These prophets foretold many events in Israelite history as well as prophesied about the birth, ministry, and death of Jesus before He was born. That is a summary of the Old Testament.

The New Testament has four gospels, each telling the story of Jesus' life on earth, a Book of Acts that give the history of the early church and focus on the life of the Apostle Paul. There are also letters (epistles) that Paul and others wrote to teach the Christian faith to new believers. It ends with the Book of Revelation, which describes the second coming of Christ.

So, Genesis 1 does not explain where God came from or when God came into existence. It simply says God existed before the beginning. I personally just accept that as fact, and I don't debate it. No one can offer proof otherwise, so I take it on faith. God then created all the other things on earth and finally created Adam and Eve. He placed them in the Garden of Eden, which was heaven on earth. There was no sin, and God lived with Adam and Eve in the Garden of Eden. They had unbroken fellowship and communion with God.

However, God also gave them free will. He did not create robots that had to love Him; He wanted His people to choose to love Him. So Adam and Eve could do what they wanted and go where they wanted, and God was always with them. However, God said there was a tree in the middle of the Garden, known as the Tree of the Knowledge of Good and Evil, and they were forbidden to eat its fruit.

The serpent (Satan) tempted Eve to eat the fruit (the Bible does not say it was an apple) from this tree, and she gave some to Adam, who also ate it. Then the Bible says their "eyes were opened." (It was the only time in history Satan told the truth!) With their eyes opened, they were like God in knowing good and evil. But by doing so, they became self-centered instead of focused on God. They went from believing, "God is our only focus" to "We can also focus on ourselves," and they instantly became self-aware. They knew they were naked.

Realizing they were naked, they hid from God in the Garden. Then Adam heard God calling for him, "Where are you?" Adam answered, "I heard you in the Garden, and I was afraid because I was naked; so, I hid." God then answered Adam, "Who told you that you were naked? Have you eaten from the tree I commanded you not to eat from?"

This is where the finger-pointing began! Adam's first response was, "The woman. It wasn't me, God. It was that woman; she's the one who ate first!" After blaming Eve, he then pointed the finger at God Himself, "It was the woman YOU gave me." If you hadn't given me that woman, Lord, none of this would have happened!

Sin had entered the world. God's creation had disobeyed His command. And there were consequences to the serpent (crawl on his belly and eat dust the rest of its life), Eve (pain in childbearing), and Adam (painful toiling to get plants from the earth). And there were consequences for you and me too. We have all inherited the sinful nature of Adam and Eve when they disobeyed God in the Garden.

Now you might think God would have put them in time-out, sent them to their room, taken away all electronic devices along with the car keys. But He didn't. Despite their disobedience, God still loved His creation. After telling them of their consequences, the first thing God did for them was to make clothes for them out of animal skins. God had compassion for humanity. Adam and Eve forfeited ever eating from the tree of life again and living forever with God in the Garden. They were banished from the Garden, forced to work the ground for food, and would begin aging and eventually die.

So, because of Adam and Eve's sin, we have all inherited their sinful nature. In addition, we will all also age and die. This created a great dilemma for God. How could God punish human sin with death, and at the same time, show His love for humanity? At first, God had the priests of the people offer blood animal sacrifices to atone for their sin on a daily basis.

This was an omen to the miracle of Passover in Egypt. When God saw blood on the doorposts, the destroying angel would pass over that house. Houses without blood on the doorpost would lose both their firstborn child and firstborn animals.

Pharaoh himself lost his firstborn son like everyone else without the blood on the doorpost. God used the blood sacrifice to foreshadow for the people that the blood would become the instrument of God's salvation—Jesus is our Passover Lamb!

But, I believe God constantly yearned for the days in the Garden. He missed the fellowship and communion with His creation in a sinless environment. The only way God could bring that experience back was to eradicate sin and create a new beginning. So, God, through Jesus Christ, became a man! Mary gave birth to Jesus in a little stable in Bethlehem with no fanfare, no marching band, no fireworks, no network coverage, and no internet streaming. It was a very humble beginning, indeed!

During Jesus' life, He performed many miracles and spoke to

thousands about the Kingdom of God. As you read the New Testament, everything you observe about Jesus reflects the character of God. You will see things like compassion, mercy, kindness, grace, forgiveness, healing, etc. These are all the same qualities seen in the Father.

Jesus told the apostle Philip, "If you have seen Me, you have seen the Father" (John 14:9). Jesus and the Father were one, which was the central characteristic of Jesus' entire ministry. He never did anything on His own; He only did what He saw the Father doing.

Simultaneously, Jesus was entirely human and experienced all the same things you and I do. So when we pray, we have the full assurance Jesus knows what we're feeling and what we're going through. He was a man too, and He can relate. He feels our pain, and He understands our anguish and fears.

Eventually the religious leaders of the day—the Pharisees—began to fear the popularity of Jesus. He was a threat to them and to the Roman rulers. Jesus had always known His Father's plan was for Him to go to the cross. God's plan to eradicate sin was to place the sins of the whole world on the shoulders of His Son. People who believed in Him, having experienced the full atonement of their sin, would receive the free gift of salvation and would be forgiven their sins.

No more sacrifices of daily blood in the Temple—Jesus' death paid the full penalty for all sins for all times! Through one man (Adam), sin entered the world; so too by one man (Jesus), sin was atoned for all people. (Romans 8:12-19).

As the time for the cross was approaching, and He was arrested by the Jewish leaders, Jesus prayed in the Garden of Gethsemane, asking His Father if His death on the cross could be avoided. He could foresee the agony of saying, "My God, my God, why have you forsaken me?" His Father said "No" and shortly thereafter, Jesus was arrested. As Jesus stood before Pontius Pilate, the local Roman governor, Pilate offered an alternative to the people. He would release one criminal, as was their custom at that time of year, either Jesus the Christ or Barabbas, a notorious criminal.

The people chose Barabbas. And God agreed with them. God's plan to redeem His people required Christ's sacrificial death on the cross. So, Jesus was crucified, died, and was buried. On the cross Jesus offered these words:

"Father, forgive them for they know not what they do." Oh, what compassion!

"Today, thou shalt be with me in paradise." Words of assurance to a dying thief on the cross next to Him.

"Woman, behold thy Son! Behold thy mother!" Words of comfort to His mother, Mary, and His apostle, John.

My God, my God, why hast thou forsaken me?" My first question when I get to heaven will be, "What happened in that moment?" My guess is the sins of the world on Christ's shoulders at that moment were more than God could bear to look at. So He turned His head away. And for the first time, Jesus felt His Father's eyes were not upon Him. It brings tears to my eyes to know my Savior suffered that abandonment for me!

"I thirst." He was totally human.

"It is finished." Notice Jesus didn't say, "I am finished." The work He came to do was done, but His resurrection was still to come.

"Father, into thy hands I commend My Spirit." The obedient Son had completed His task, and He would soon be reunited with His Father.

Jesus was placed in a tomb and a large stone was rolled in front to seal it. Guards were placed at the tomb to prevent anyone from stealing the body. They had heard Jesus predict He would rise from the grave. But the very thing they were sent there to prevent, they confirmed. On the third day, Jesus rose from the dead, just as He had predicted to His disciples.

He appeared to Mary and Martha and then to the disciples in bodily form. Thomas had to touch the nail holes in His hands before he would believe. But afterward he said," My Lord and My God!" Thomas immediately went from believing "Nobody rises from the dead" to "This man was the Son of God!"

Before ascending to heaven, Jesus told the disciples He would be sending the Comforter (The Holy Spirit) who would teach them all things. On the Day of Pentecost, the Holy Spirit descended on the disciples. And this event changed them forever. Instead of His presence *with* them, it was now His presence *in* them. And for us, who were never with Him in the flesh, receiving the Holy Spirit upon salvation changes everything!

God's plan of salvation was complete. Christ came and died on the cross for our sins. Forgiveness is God's free gift to us—to all who believe. In Romans 10:9, Paul says, "If you declare with your mouth, 'Jesus is Lord,' and believe in your heart that God raised Him from the dead, you will be saved."

In John's Gospel 3:16 it says. "For God so loved the world that He gave His one and only Son; that whoever believes in Him will not perish, but have eternal life." Now, look at that verse again and put your name in as a substitute for the words "the world"—for God so loved YOUR NAME, that He gave His one and only Son, that whoever (that's you, pal) believes in Him will not perish, but will have eternal life."

So, there you have the whole Bible in *Cliff Notes*. God loves you. He loves you enough to give His only Son for you. It is a free gift. All you have to do is believe it in your heart and the gift of salvation is yours. We serve a risen Savior. He is Alive!

The lyrics to *He's Alive,* written by Don Francisco, tells the story of Peter during the three days before Jesus rose from the dead. It is a fitting way to close this chapter. Here is the code to access that song on the internet:

https://youtu.be/4Lmv_xR6_q8

FOR PERSONAL REFLECTION AND DISCUSSION

- Do you find the Bible hard to understand? Why or why not?
- What have you done to improve your understanding of the Bible?
- What do you tell others is the essential message of the Bible?

14

How Good Is Good Enough?

I hated teachers in high school who graded tests on a curve. I preferred a straight scale of:

A was 90-100%
B was 80-89%
C was 70-79%
D was 60-69%
F was anything below 60

Grading on a curve meant my grade was dependent on what everyone else scored. If I got a 73 on a test, that might be the highest score in the class, or it might be the lowest score. You never knew what was good enough!

Many people believe that good people go to heaven, which seems to make sense on a human level. Some people think God keeps a list of our good acts along with a list of our bad ones. They believe if their good list is longer than their bad one, they will go to heaven.

So my question to those people is always, "How good is good enough?" Is 83% the cut-off point? Or do you have to be in the 90th percentile to get into heaven? Or is it just 51%? What would it say about a teacher who told you that you must do well on your exam to pass but didn't tell you what score was required to pass? And what would it say about a god who told you to be good but didn't tell you "how good is good enough" to go to heaven?

Fortunately, heaven and hell have nothing to do with how good or bad you are. There are both good and bad people in both heaven and hell. The criterion for entering heaven is whether you believe Jesus Christ died for your sins on the cross. Jesus said, "I am the way, the truth, and the life. No one comes to the Father but by me" (John 14:6).

The only way to heaven is by accepting Christ as your Lord and Savior. This may not seem right or fair by human standards, but that doesn't mean it isn't true. God says, "My thoughts are not your thoughts, neither are your ways My ways" (Isaiah 55:8).

Getting into heaven isn't going to be based on what you think is right or fair. There are "bad" people in heaven—King David committed both murder and adultery; Peter denied and swore he didn't know Jesus; the woman was taken in adultery; Paul declared himself to be the chief among sinners; and me, who probably isn't too far behind Paul. And there are certainly "good" people in hell—those that never accepted Jesus. Rest assured, you will go somewhere after you die, and Jesus is the pivotal point that decides your destination.

I'm not going to heaven because I'm good, and I'm not going to hell because I'm bad. But I'm for sure going to one of those two places. And what I decide to do about Jesus makes all the difference in my destination.

It is a common belief if you join and/or are baptized in a particular church denomination, attend faithfully, put money in the collection plate each Sunday, and do good things, then you will go to heaven. The fallacy in that belief is that true Christianity is a relationship—not a membership! Matthew 7:21-23 says that just because you obey the law and go to church, etc., doesn't mean that you are saved.

Jesus explicitly says only the one who does the will of His Father in heaven will enter heaven. The will of the Father is to accept His gift of salvation created through the death and resurrection of His beloved Son—asking Jesus to be the Lord of your life and being born again. The most terrifying verse in the Bible is verse 23: "and then I will declare to them, I never knew you; depart from me, you who practice lawlessness!"

In Luke 15, there is a story of the rich man and Lazarus. The rich man, in hell, looks to heaven and asks Father Abraham if He would send Lazarus with some water to quench the fire. Look carefully now at the second half of God's answer, "And besides all this, between us and you a great chasm has been set in place, so that those who want to go from here to you cannot, nor can anyone cross over from there to us." The great chasm between heaven and hell is fixed. Neither can cross to the other side. Game over! The time to decide was while they were living.

At the end of that story, the rich man asked Abraham to send Lazarus back to tell his brothers about hell so they won't end up there with him. God again says no, "They have Moses and the prophets, let them listen to them." But the rich man says, "No, but if someone goes back from the dead they will repent." Again, God says they won't listen even if someone rises from the dead. The irony is Jesus did raise someone named Lazarus from the dead (John 11). And Jesus Himself was raised from the dead, and still people don't believe. The diagram below shows what this chasm might look like:

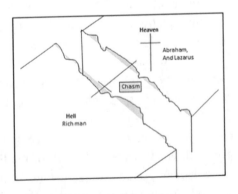

The chasm separates heaven from hell. God says that after death, no one can cross the chasm in either direction. Before death, however, the chasm is breached by the cross. The cross lies across the chasm, allowing those accepting Christ's death on the cross to bridge the chasm and be assured of heaven.

The Bible tells us that the way is narrow, "Enter through the narrow gate. For wide is the gate and broad is the road that leads to destruction, and many enter through it. But small is the gate and narrow the road that leads to life and only a few find it" (Matthew 7: 13-14). And in Matthew 25, Jesus tells a similar story about separating the sheep from the goats. The sheep go to the right (heaven) and the goats to the left (hell). So be a sheep and take the narrow road and the narrow gate.

We have all sinned and fallen short of God's glory. Salvation is not works-based, meaning based on your performance. Salvation is totally faith-based. And your faith in Jesus Christ is the narrow way. So follow the sheep.

There is a story I heard from Joel Barker and his work on the power of vision. He spoke of an older man who lived near the Pacific Ocean and how each morning he went out to the beach to begin his day with meditation. He saw a person in the distance who appeared to be dancing. He was curious and walked toward this person. As he got closer, he realized the person wasn't dancing. A young man was picking something up off the beach and throwing it back into the ocean.

He asked the young man what he was doing. He replied, "I'm throwing starfish back into the ocean. The tide is going out and the sun is coming up, and if I don't, they'll die." The man told him, "Young man, there are miles of beach, and the starfish are everywhere. You can't possibly make a difference." The young man picked up another starfish, threw it into the ocean, and said, "It made a difference for that one!" And, of course, he was right. It's important to make a difference, even if it's only for one person.

Maybe you're the one person this book was written for. Maybe you're the one person who believes you are "good enough." But what if you're wrong and you end up not being good enough? Fortunately, this life isn't a test. It's not about being good enough. It's like a baseball game—you either have a ticket, or you don't. That's the criteria for getting into the game. Jesus is your ticket for getting into heaven. You either have Him, or you don't. So, quit trying to be good, and just get your ticket.

FOR PERSONAL REFLECTION AND DISCUSSION

- Do you believe good people will go to heaven? Why, why not?
- What determines where you spend eternity?
- What do you see as the urgent imperative represented by the chasm between heaven and hell?

15

Is God Punishing Me?

I remember when my friend, Jack, came back from Vietnam. During his deployment, he had killed a pregnant Vietnamese woman who was carrying explosives in a basket and headed toward a group of his buddies. He shot and killed her before she could detonate her explosives. But Jack had a lot of trouble dealing with what he had done, and that raw memory stayed with him for a long time. Years later, his first child was born with Down syndrome, and Jack truly believed it was because he had killed that pregnant woman in Vietnam, and God was punishing him.

You may have known people in your life who thought God was punishing them for something they had done. Maybe you know people with similar war stories or those who were guilty of vehicular homicide and later believed God was punishing them for what they had done. Some people get cancer and believe God gave it to them because of something they had done earlier in their life. People walk around with tremendous guilt over things they have done in their past. I have good news for all those people, and perhaps for you!

God doesn't punish you for what you've done! All the punishment for sin was placed on the shoulders of His Son when He died on the cross. We've all sinned, and God made provision for the forgiveness of our sins at the cross. Accepting Christ's death on the cross as the punishment for your sin is what salvation is all about. Christ paid your debt permanently. Nothing is more liberating than knowing your sins are forgiven, and God is not punishing you.

The devil is the "accuser" of all mankind and seeks our destruction. He will never let you forget one second of what you did in the past. He will continually pile guilt upon your troubled soul. Psalm 103:12 says that when we confess our sins and accept His salvation, "as far as the east is from the west, so far has He removed our transgressions from us" and remembers them no more. Satan will use anything he can to keep you from a relationship with a forgiving God.

However, there are always real consequences of sin. But there is a big difference between consequences and punishment. For example, if a man commits adultery and contracts a sexually transmitted disease, and then gives that disease to his wife, there will be consequences.

But as a Christian, after confessing and genuinely repenting of your sin with a broken and contrite heart, God will forgive you. Your wife may not, but God will. God will not punish you for your transgression. The consequences may be divorce, and you'll have to live with those consequences, but it won't be punishment from God.

Some people cheat on their taxes, and when they get caught, they may go to jail. But jail is the consequence of the cheating, not God punishing them. Recently, there was a college cheating scandal where wealthy Hollywood parents paid large sums of money to get their children fraudulently into the college of their choice. They got caught, and now they're paying the consequences. But God is not punishing them.

We all sin and must face the consequences of our sin. But when we accept Christ as our Savior and recognize His death paid the price for our sin, we can accept God's gift of forgiveness. That is your salvation! You need not fear any further punishment from God. Jesus paid it all.

When we sin, we often feel remorse and beat ourselves up because we are disappointed in ourselves. Joyce remembers someone who could not forgive herself. A wise counselor told her friend that by not forgiving herself, she was, in fact, saying that Jesus' death on the cross was not enough! What an eye-opener! First John 1:9 says that "if we confess our sins, God is faithful and just to forgive us our sins and to cleanse us from all unrighteousness!" At that point, our fellowship with God is immediately restored, and our eternal love relationship with Him continues.

So it doesn't matter what you've done; God will forgive you. Jesus died for you and took all the punishment you deserved. Accepting Him as your Savior means eternal life. It means freedom to love and serve God for what He has done for you. God is about love and forgiveness, not punishment. So if you think God is punishing you, then you have another thing coming. God loves you; He is not punishing you." John 3:16 says,

> For God so loved you, that He gave His only Son, that when you believe in Him you will not perish but have everlasting life.

If God isn't punishing you, isn't it time you stopped punishing yourself? Jesus is waiting for you to come home, just like the Prodigal Son!

FOR PERSONAL REFLECTION AND DISCUSSION

- Have you ever thought God was punishing you? Describe
- How do you see the difference between punishment and consequences?
- Describe a time when you've seen the consequences of sin (in yourself or others).

16

Becoming

Regardless of our age, all of us are constantly in some form of becoming. We're becoming older, or smarter, or better, or taller, or fatter, or something. We are always evolving, changing, and becoming someone different. Most of us want to be better at something—a better student, better athlete, better parent, better spouse, or a better friend. We're always in the process of becoming something different than we were yesterday. And I think that is a good thing.

At some point in time, most people think about marriage. Some people like the idea of marriage and the concept of a life partner and perhaps a family. Others consider marriage and reject the idea outright. But even those who reject the concept of marriage usually like the idea of dating and companionship.

This chapter has some guidelines for single people who have decided marriage is something they would like to pursue and are searching for a mate. So, the $64,000 question is—for what kind of person are you looking? Most people seeking a mate have a list of qualities they're looking for—smart, attractive, athletic, spiritual, wealthy, etc.

And the second question is—are you going to the places where those type of people hang out? If you're looking for an athletic person, have you joined a gym? If you're looking for an avid reader, have you joined a book club or library? If you're looking for a spiritual person, have you joined a church? You need to be in the places where the person you're looking for can be found.

Eventually, the qualities you are looking for will begin to mature. You become concerned with more fundamental attributes like:

- Are they kind?
- Are they loving?
- Are they considerate?
- Are they spiritual?
- Are they thoughtful?
- Are they generous?
- Are they compassionate?
- Do they value the same things I do?
- Do they enjoy the same things I do?
- Do they want a family?
- What do they want to be doing in 10 years? 20 years?
- Do they want to get married or just date with no commitment?
- Do they have the same monetary goals and spending habits?
- Do they take care of themselves physically?

Usually after some dating (maybe even the first date), you begin to eliminate people who don't have the qualities you desire. As soon as I discovered some character flaw or saw that a required attribute was lacking, I never dated a person again. What was the point? I would never marry such a person. That's not to say they were terrible—they just weren't for me.

So let me assume for a moment you know what kind of person you're looking to find. But what is that person looking for? If you want to marry that type of person, then you need to be what that type of person is looking for, right? You need to be the person that the person you're looking for is desiring to find!

If you become that person, then they will find you because they're looking for you as much as you're looking for them. If you're looking for someone kind, then be kind. If you're looking for someone generous, then be generous. If you're looking for someone smart, then become smart. If you're looking for someone godly, then be godly. Make sense?

One Sunday, my pastor told a story about a family he knew quite well. They were God-fearing people and went to church every week. They had a daughter who became a Christian in her early teens. When she graduated from high school, she went off to the University of Georgia. Soon she began attending fraternity parties, drinking beer, and hanging out with people who enjoyed that kind of lifestyle. Then she eventually became sexually active with a guy and soon began sleeping around.

She would come home from time to time, and her mom would ask her how things were going. She was honest with her mom and told her all the things going on in her life. Her mom asked if she was going to church, but of course, she wasn't going to church anymore.

Then one year she came home for the Christmas holidays and went to a party with some friends. The next morning at breakfast, she was all excited to tell her mom what had happened. She said, "Mom, you're not going to believe what happened. I met this guy. He is soooo good looking. He has a great job, he drives a really nice car, he makes a lot of money, and he just bought his first house. And Mom, he is so nice. And guess what else? You're not going to believe this—he's a Christian. Aren't you excited for me?"

Her mom then turned to her and said, "That's just great, honey. There's only one problem. A boy like that isn't looking for a girl like you." Whoa! It must have been difficult for the mom to have to say that to her daughter, and even more difficult for the daughter to hear it. But the truth doesn't hurt unless it ought to.

It's all about you, and being the best person you can be. They will find you. My advice to my daughters was to seek first a godly man. In my experience, a godly man will exhibit more of the qualities she is looking for in a husband and will be more likely to be a good father as well.

It is important to understand what marriage actually means. It is not about passion, warm fuzzies, or fun times. Most couples who are engaged and planning their wedding are often more excited about the location, the food, the entertainment, the perfect dress, etc., than the commitment they will be making in front of witnesses. Some choose to quietly exchange vows before a Justice of the Peace and skip the wedding extravaganza all together.

The concept of marriage is God's idea, which is outlined in Genesis 2:18, 21-24. His concept of marriage is not a contract but rather a covenant between a man and a woman in the sight of God, which lasts until death when they part ways. How can you know you can spend the rest of your life with the same spouse in good times and in bad times, in sickness and in health, for richer or for poorer? You can't predict the future, and there is no guarantee you will be together until death parts you from your spouse.

All marriages have their seasons—the honeymoon, the children (which lasts for the rest of your life), the empty nest, and the golden years. During each stage, all kinds of things can occur—separation because of military service, a terminal illness, loss of a job, financial hardships, etc. Can love overcome all of these and survive? The thing to focus on and pray about is this commitment for the rest of your life. What a sobering thought!!

A Word About Divorce

Both Joyce and I have both been divorced and have remarried. Our current marriages, with Jesus as the third strand of our covenants with our spouses, have stood the test of time. I have been married to Sherrie for 36 years. Joyce has been married to Peter for 26 years. When the heartbreak of divorce happened, we each had to go back to square one.

Everyone has broken relationships in their past, and the important details of why that relationship failed have to be reviewed and dealt with before you are able to return to seeking a lifelong spouse. What did we do to each other that caused the breakup? You need to find truthful answers to these questions, as uncomfortable as they may be, and learn from your mistakes. The biggest and most challenging thing for Joyce to do was to forgive her former spouse.

Because of extending circumstances, which Joyce writes about in another chapter, they didn't have the biblical commitment of covenant because neither of them had a relationship with the Lord at that time. For me, the divorce wasn't about forgiveness because I don't think either of us did anything wrong—we just grew apart. I struggled with wondering if I had made the right decision.

Since both Joyce and I had children from our first marriages, it was imperative to us that our children continue to love and respect our former spouses, their biological parents. Getting remarried is a more difficult undertaking because you are not only marrying your new spouse, but you are a "package deal," including your children (and perhaps their children) if you are the custodial parent.

Note that it is much more difficult if your new spouse has been widowed and has grieving children. The most critical thing that needs to be established is you are NOT replacing the deceased parent but are a supplemental parent to love them into adulthood. That was Joyce's biggest challenge because Peter was a widower with two grown children and a teenager when he married her. She and Peter loved each other's children as their own. Since they were married, Peter's oldest son and Joyce's only child, a son, have died. They equally shared the sorrow.

When Sherrie and I got married, we each had custody of our two children. Putting four teenagers together didn't result in the Brady Bunch. In our vows, we promised to love each other's children as our own. For 36 years, we have both been true to that vow. Another vow we made to each other was no problem in our marriage would ever be bigger than our love and commitment to each other. That promise took every thought of "not reconciling a difference" off the table. We were committed to each other and committed to working through any problem.

In today's society, many people who have been divorced or widowed are looking for a new spouse. Some are young, and others are older, in their forties or fifties. There are also seniors who have lost their lifelong spouse and are looking for love and companionship.

It is important to try to get it right the first time! It's critical to understand and accept the concept of covenant where each spouse gives the other 100 percent in all things. So, if you're looking for the perfect spouse, then also consider what Jesus said, "Seek first the Kingdom of God and His righteousness, and all these things will be added to you as well." Become the person that the person you're looking for desires. It starts with you, and it's about becoming!

It is appropriate to close this chapter with a song recorded years ago by a group called Peter, Paul, and Mary. It is titled the Wedding Song. The words are really powerful! Here is the code to access the song on the Internet:

https://youtu.be/hR051uCNrAw

FOR PERSONAL REFLECTION AND DISCUSSION

- If/when you were single, what were you looking for in a spouse?
- Would the spouse you are (or were) looking for be interested in you? Why?
- Why do you think divorce rates are so high today?

17

God Owes Me Nothing

I saw a video recently on YouTube of a small Asian boy whose mother was very sick. He went to the market to get food for her, but he didn't have enough money. A kind woman shop owner saw his dilemma and gave him a free bag of soup. Years later, that little boy became a doctor. And the kind woman who had given him a free bag of soup was in the hospital.

The doctor recognized her, operated on her, and helped her get well. As she was leaving, the hospital presented her with a billing statement. On the bill, the doctor had written, "You owe me nothing—paid for with one bag of soup many years ago." We can tell God the same thing, "You owe me nothing."

Over the past several generations, many young people's life philosophy has been based on the concept of entitlement in all its shapes and sizes. Over time, these entitlements became their personal rights, and everyone was expected to respect them because "mankind owes me." Going to the extreme, this philosophy crosses over to their belief that God owes them everything!

When we begin to grow up, we experience identifiable and universal rites of passage—sleeping through the night, rolling over, sitting up, sucking your thumb, cutting baby teeth, creeping on the floor, standing up, running, and potty training. Once we became somewhat self-sufficient, we craved to become independent and establish our own kingdom of self with ourselves seated on the throne.

We became little tyrants during our terrible twos and rebelled against doing anything our parents wanted us to do. We learned by trial and error how to get our parents to do what we wanted and memorized that universal word "no" to get our own way.

As we navigated the terrible twos, we would win little victories against our parents' control. Over time, our resulting entitlement arsenal began to grow. When we emerged from the terrible twos and went to school and shared things, we had to put our entitlements on hold for a while. However, by this time, the concept was permanently branded on our personalities.

As we grew into adulthood, we became products of our parents' ability to successfully parent us. Some of us came from broken homes, some of us had serious illnesses, some of our parents lost jobs, and some of us were bullied or marginalized. All these life situations were like being a raw diamond and having nut shells buffet us to create facets on the polished diamond at the end of the process.

By the time we were eighteen or so, our outlook on life was pretty well defined. Some ideas emerged like, "The world owes me a living," "Nothing is my fault," and "I don't have to do anything you say because you can't tell me what to do."

But the wonderful truth is we have a loving Father who showers us with His love and mercies. He is Almighty God!! He doesn't owe us anything —we owe Him everything!

Because God is love personified, He created you with your unique gifts and abilities in His image. He thought up a perfect plan for your life to use them to fulfill the hopes and dreams in your life. The most precious gift He gave you was Jesus Christ, His only Son, to live and die in your place for your sins so you could be forgiven and made whole again. He didn't have to do that, but He loves you so much He made that sacrifice for you. Who could ask for anything more?

As you begin to see God in His true perspective, you can only marvel in awe at what He has done for you because of His great love. When I realized this in my own life, my only response was to fall on my knees and thank Him! He didn't owe me this gift of salvation—Jesus paid the ultimate price for me—He would have gone to the cross if I were the only person on this earth! That boggles my mind and makes me feel so insignificant. How could I dare demand anything of God?

By His grace, I have learned not to demand things from God but to humbly ask Him for my needs and the needs of others in humble prayer. I abdicated the throne of self and placed Jesus on the throne of my life forever—what a happy and wondrous that day was!

God made each of us unique and gave us distinct and special talents and skills so we can love Him above all things. We can follow the plan He has for us to give us a future and a hope! Our special gift from God is our free will, allowing us choices in our lives that only we can make but bringing consequences for wrong choices. He leaves the decision up to each one. My heart is full and my heart sings. All I have and all I am belongs to God for He saved me! Thank You, Father God!

FOR PERSONAL REFLECTION AND DISCUSSION

- Do you think there is a big entitlement mentality today? Why, why not?
- Do you think God owes you? Why, why not?
- What do people think God most owes them?

18

Life and Gender Choices

We are blessed to live in a country where we enjoy God-given rights specified in the Bill of Rights to the U.S. Constitution. These rights include freedom of speech, freedom of religion, the bearing of arms (gun ownership), etc. Our Founding Fathers covered the basics in establishing a new nation based on the laws of God found in the Bible.

The Supreme Court established the right to have an abortion on January 22, 1973 in the famous Roe versus Wade court case. It is interesting to note that this ruling by the Supreme Court occurred before the science of sonograms was publicly available. Mothers can now actually see their fetus in the womb! Perhaps that technology (and newer technology) may affect future court rulings if Roe v. Wade is ever revisited by the Supreme Court.

This Supreme Court decision allows a woman to have a legal, secular right to abort her child. But God has a totally different take on this subject.

In Genesis 2:7 (NASB), God created man out of dust from the ground and breathed into his nostrils the breath of life, and the man became a living being. In Genesis 2:21-22 (NASB), God caused the man to go into a deep sleep and removed one of his ribs and created woman out of it.

In creating man and woman, God gave them the gift of procreation—being able to bear children and populate the earth. When creating man, God said, "Let us make man in Our image, according to Our likeness. God created man in His own image, in the image of God; male and female He created them" (Genesis 1:26-27 NASB).

The purpose of the man and the woman was to form a covenant together with God and be blessed with children to fill the earth and subdue it. God thus decreed that children were a gift from Him as part of the covenant established above. Psalm 127:3 (NASB) says that children are a gift of the Lord. The fruit of the womb is a reward! James 1:17 (NASB) states," Every good thing given and every perfect gift is from above, coming down from the Father of lights, with whom there is no variation or shifting shadow."

Children are a gift from the Lord! Psalm 139 makes clear that

You formed my inward parts; You wove me in my mother's womb. I will give thanks to You, for I am fearfully and wonderfully made; wonderful are Your works and my soul knows it very well. My frame was not hidden from You when I was made in secret and skillfully wrought in the depths of the earth; Your eyes have seen my unformed substance; and in Your book were all written the days ordained for me, when as yet there was not one of them (Psalm 139:13-16 NASB).

These scriptures state how God sees a fetus in the womb as a miracle of creation and a precious gift. Every person since Adam and Eve was formed in their mother's womb, and all mankind shares that incredible fact. You wouldn't be here today if your mother had decided to abort you!

Whether the child is conceived by rape, incest, or miscalculating her fertile period, a woman's child lives and grows in her womb, sustains life through the umbilical cord, hears his/her mother's heartbeat, and is a living, dynamic person who feels pain and other stimuli.

It's interesting to note also that death is proclaimed by a doctor when a heartbeat no longer exists. Yet life is not declared to exist by pro-choice advocates when a heartbeat is initially detected. If it is the absence of heartbeat that determines death, shouldn't the presence of a heartbeat determine life? If a pregnant woman is murdered, why do prosecutors charge the murderer with double homicide? They recognize the fact that the fetus is alive, and they charge the offender with double homicide. So, does that make abortion a homicide—only the mother gets to live? Something to ponder.

Many women today long to conceive a child, but they are physically unable to conceive or to carry a baby to term. Many of them would be more than willing to adopt your child.

God sees life as a cause to celebrate the miracle He has given you, and you should cherish His gift. It's not a choice; it's a life. Before you think, "It's my body, therefore it's my choice," consider who gave you your life. God has a vested interest in you, and you should consult with Him first before you make that decision. Ultimately it is your decision—hopefully, you will choose life for your child.

Another trend suggests there are more than two genders out there and that we can choose what gender we want to be based on how we feel and how we see ourselves.

God says that in the beginning, He created male and female genders, period. Somehow in our childhoods, the notion of boy versus girl has become muddled. Children's emotions grow right alongside their bodies, and hormones kick in on the way to adulthood. Each stage of development—pre-school, elementary school, 'tween, teenager, young adult—is experienced differently from child to child.

God does not make mistakes—He created every child with its gifts, talents, dreams, and abilities in His own image! To Him, gender identity is fixed at the time the child is conceived! It may help to talk with a counselor or good friend about your feelings and pray to God for guidance that you can grasp what God created you to be in His plan for your life!

The last topic in this chapter relates to gender preference. The Bible teaches that homosexuality is considered a sin against God's written Word. God created man and woman so there could be the ability to love and cherish each other and to procreate children (Genesis 1:28 NASB). God didn't create another male partner for Adam. If the whole world were homosexual, then human life would eventually end because a man cannot conceive and give birth. God made a woman to do that part of procreation, and it was His intention that she would do so.

But God loves homosexuals, and so should we. As members of mankind, every person is a sinner; therefore, we do not have the right to judge people just because they sin differently from us. Our task is to tell them about Jesus. The Holy Spirit will deal with the issues about their sexuality.

Steve commented about a gay pride march in Atlanta, Georgia, that went past Charles Stanley's Baptist Church. Some people held up signs protesting the gay march, but the church across the street handed out water bottles. Which church gave the protestors a drink of cold water, and which church judged them? Which side of the street do you think Jesus would have been on?

In every topic in this chapter, it is critical to understand that God loves the sinner but hates the sin. Each man and woman is made in the image of Almighty God and assigned to follow God's moral laws regarding their manhood or womanhood. God does not make mistakes in assigning gender. He is adamant that sexual relationships between men/men and women/women are not His perfect plan and are an abomination to His holy Word. He also considers abortion as murder.

Abortion, gender change, and homosexuality will always be divisive and explosive issues. The Good News is God loves all people equally because He sent His only Son, Jesus Christ, to die for each person's past, present, and future sins. God is more than able to forgive any sin, but the sinner must exercise his/her free will and choose to change their lifestyle through His abiding and enabling grace.

Know that Jesus can heal your body, mind, and soul from all past experiences if you accept Him into your life. His yoke is easy, and His burden is light. Come and see that the Lord is good! Come and see "things which eye has not seen and ear has not heard, and which have not entered the heart of man, all that God has prepared for those who love Him (1 Corinthians 2:9 NASB)!

In closing, let me say that Steve and I believe God's Word to be truth. The Bible is very specific about abortion, homosexuality, and gender. But regardless of the choices you may have made in the past, God does not condemn you. God forgives! Like the Prodigal Son, decide to come home. A loving Father awaits you.

FOR PERSONAL REFLECTION AND DISCUSSION

- Is there a situation where abortion is acceptable to you? Explain.
- If so, does that make you pro-choice? Why or why not?
- In your opinion, what has caused the homosexuality, gender identity, and sexual preference phenomenon in our country?

19

Earning Forgiveness

You may remember the old financial investment commercial that said, "We make money the old-fashioned way—we earn it." And we learn growing up that earning things is a good and respected way to live. Whatever we get in life, we must earn it. And it makes sense from a human perspective. It varies greatly from the entitlement mentality so prevalent in America today.

But unfortunately for us, we can't earn anything from God. You can't earn your way to heaven, and you can't earn favor with God. God views us as lost and unable to earn anything because of our sin. But, fortunately, God also loves us! Therefore, He chose to make a provision for our sins. He sent His Son to die on a cross to pay the penalty for our sins. We can't earn it—it is a gift from God.

Our salvation comes in believing Christ died for us. It is our faith in Him that saves us. Paul says in Ephesians 2:8,

For it is by grace you have been saved, through faith—and this is not of yourselves, it is a gift from God—not by works (earning), so that no one can boast.

Salvation is a gift from God that cannot be earned. No one can boast about their works or how they earned salvation.

How many times have you seen or heard about some wonder product or stock investment opportunity or sweepstakes offer? What about a free trip to somewhere including hotel and airfare because you are special? Your first impression is usually, "It's too good to be true!" Our gut feelings respond to such promotions are

"Yeah, right! What's the catch?" Many naïve people have been deceived by believing what these promotions say. They hope this promotion will be the answer in their life, especially in a time of sickness or financial hardship.

When we are weak, we become more gullible to these ploys, and unfortunately, we are ultimately left to deal with the consequences of our misplaced trust and folly. We have been conned, scammed, and used by sly, greedy, dishonest people who earn their living by destroying others' hopes and dreams for their own financial gain. The underlying result of such an experience is often huge personal loss, leaving us with paranoia about anything that seems too easy. As the saying goes, "If it's too good to be true, then it probably is!"

These encounters leave us cynical and untrusting about anything. It confirms there is no such thing as a free lunch. It seeps into everything we see and do and builds up a spirit of suspicion and skepticism in our daily lives. For example, because of all the misinformation and rumors abounding across the country about Covid, we are confused on whom to trust, if anybody, and what to do to prevent the spread of the virus we know very little about.

This skepticism is a deadly foe—it can destroy our relationships with our friends and neighbors. Some people are paid to snitch on others who don't wear masks or practice social distancing. We have become germophobic about public places and don't know what to do to be truly safe.

This skepticism can cross over to our spiritual lives as well. The concept that "grace is too easy—that's it's all you need to be forgiven" is laughable to many of us. "C'mon! I must have to do something to earn it! Hmm, I promise to visit every sick person I know and help old people cross the street. I won't cheat on my taxes anymore, and I'll give up sweets for Lent.

"Maybe all that will make me eligible to earn God's grace for myself! Oh no, wait! What about my spouse and my kids? What extra things do I have to do to get God's grace for them? Then there is my mother-in-law—Umm, I think I'll let her earn her own grace!"

Sadly, this is the understanding of many people about any gift from God. They can't see Him because He is Spirit and can't hear Him because they do not have spiritual ears to hear. They can't touch Him because He is not a used car salesman or a celebrity endorsing a brand of car insurance.

Grace is not a "pay-it-forward" behavior either, where you pay for grace for the person behind you in line, like a family member. While God's grace is free to us, it was not cheap for God. It cost God the physical death of His beloved Son, Jesus Christ, on a cross outside the city of Jerusalem.

Jesus paid the price, once for all mankind, to be able to offer gifts of grace and salvation to everyone in the whole world for all time. It was the most expensive gift in history! So, while free to us, it cost God everything! He sacrificed totally of Himself and His love to give us the gift of salvation.

So, there you have it—God's amazing grace is FREE for the asking! Nothing to earn! Like the latest Turbo Tax commercial says, "It's free, free, free, free!" So, get your grace and salvation the old-fashioned way—accept it for free!

FOR PERSONAL REFLECTION AND DISCUSSION

- Do you feel you need to earn forgiveness? Why, why not?
- In your opinion, when does a gift become a gift? When is it given? When is it received? When is it opened? When do you own it as yours? Discuss.
- If you have to earn something, is it really a gift? Explain.

20

God Actually Loves Me

In my youth, I went through difficult situations in my family, and my self-worth was calculated in negative numbers. I couldn't love myself because I thought I was damaged goods. After some wild living, at twenty-five, I married my first husband. I became a mother three years later, and then everything fell apart totally in my life.

When my husband left me with a 10-month-old son, I was considering ending it all. One day a close friend came over for lunch and introduced me to Jesus, and I gave my life to Him that very day, forty-three years ago. I was loved unconditionally by my Father in heaven, but it took many years for me to begin to love myself!

God has created people with tremendous differences in personalities. There are bubbly people and quiet people, happy people and angry people, activists and peacemakers, doers and thinkers, courageous and cowardly people. God has made each person in His image. I am a favorite child of God with promise and endless possibilities as I walk out the plan for my life that He created just for me!

This promise is God's stamp of approval of each person He has created. Healthy personalities have the courage and tenacity to be all they want to be and have a healthy outlook on life. They accept who they are and go and make the most of what life has to offer. They use all of the gifts and talents God gave them, and they "go for it"!

However, there are also people like me, whose spirit has been broken by life's circumstances, and their self-worth is very low. They have zero confidence in their gifts and talents because they don't believe in themselves. Perhaps this mindset was created by PTSD (Post Traumatic Stress Disorder) when something overly traumatic happened to them. This mental state is considered a mental illness.

It happens not only to military personnel and veterans but also to others—abused children, battered spouses, or adults who experienced other physical phenomena that scared them to death. In time, most people are reconciled to the disasters or tragedies they have experienced, but mentally fragile people lose even more hope in living successfully, and some completely withdraw from life itself. They rarely go out of their homes or speak to others. They become hermits of self-pity and despair, afraid their lives will never change because they cannot love themselves. So tragic, but there is hope!

Wikipedia defines depression as: "A state of low mood and aversion to activity. It affects a person's thought, behavior, motivation, feelings and sense of well-being." Sadness is a normal reaction to life events. Clinical depression, however, is a serious disease and usually involves counseling and possibly medical treatment in order to be controlled.

When the situation is treated, the depression often fades, and the person can resume a normal lifestyle. But if this mental viewpoint goes untreated, some people become totally convinced no one can love them or care for them at all. Even God doesn't love them because they cannot love themselves!

But God's good news is you are so special to Him that He sent Jesus to die for your sins. He would have done that if you were the only person on earth. God loves and delights in His children and has a special plan for your life! Jeremiah 29:11 (NASB) says, "For I know the plans that I have for you," declares the Lord, "plans for welfare and not for calamity to give you a future and a hope!"

Regarding Jesus, Isaiah 42:3 (NASB) says that "a bruised reed He will not break and a dimly burning wick He will not extinguish." Jesus is there to pick you up and to restore you in your body, mind, and spirit.

The devil's devious strategy is to keep you hating yourself and avoiding God at all costs! He uses this negative self-image for his destructive purposes, paralyzing you so you can't think for yourself. You are like an insect caught in the devil's spider web.

The blood of Jesus wipes out the devil's spider webs and any other hold the devil has on your life. The gift of salvation sets you free to be all God made you to be! You have a choice. You can believe what you feel (unworthy of love), or you can believe what God says about you—that He loves you. In my book, what God says cancels out what I feel every time.

Your life definitely matters to God, and like a little girl once said, "I know I'm somebody 'cause God don't make no junk!" Look into the hopes and dreams, gifts and talents He gave you when He created you and know that it is okay to love yourself through His eyes! You once were lost, but now you're found; you were blind, but now you can see. You are no longer a wretch in His sight (or yours) because His amazing grace has set you free! Now I am set free forever! Amen!

FOR PERSONAL REFLECTION AND DISCUSSION

• Have you ever felt unloved? Describe.
• How do you know your life really matters to God?

21

I Can See Clearly Now

Many people in history have started out as bad people but then changed and became outstanding people. One of the most notorious is Oskar Schindler. They made a movie about him called Schindler's List. He was born in what is now the Czech Republic. He was not a saint for he cheated on his wife, drank excessively, and spied for the Germans. Eager to make money, he set up a factory exploiting Jewish and Polish workers. Over time he began to see the Jews not just as cheap labor but as mothers, fathers, and children exposed to ruthless slaughter. During World War II, he is credited with saving the lives of more than 1,200 Jews.

In the Bible, the Apostle Paul made a similar turnaround in his life. Saul of Tarsus, later called Paul the Apostle, had an intimidating reputation in the early days of the infant Church and was zealous about pursuing and imprisoning Christians! His resume was quite impressive:

Although I myself might have confidence even in the flesh.
If anyone else has a mind to put confidence in the flesh, I
far more: circumcised on the eighth day, of the nation of
Israel, of the tribe of Benjamin, a Hebrew of Hebrews; as
to the law, a Pharisee; as to zeal, a persecutor of the
church, as to righteousness which is found in the Law,
found blameless (Philippians 3:4-6 NASB).

He felt he was superior to all other people, and he acted accordingly!

Saul was determined to punish and get rid of anyone who offended the traditional Jewish Law. In Paul's day, men treated women as personal property, and the self-righteous Jews of that era excluded disabled people, lepers, and others.

The Damascus Road experience is found in Acts 9:1-22 (NASB). Paul encountered the Lord through a bright flash of light from heaven, which made him fall to the ground where he heard a voice saying to him, "Saul, Saul, why are you persecuting Me?" And Paul said, "Who are You, Lord? And Jesus said, "I am Jesus whom you are persecuting, but get up and enter the city, and it will be told you what you must do" (Acts 9:3-6 NASB). The men who traveled with him were speechless because they heard the voice of Jesus but saw no one.

When Saul got up from the ground, he was blind, humiliated, and bewildered and had to be led into Damascus, where he stayed for three days, no doubt perplexed and dumbfounded in his present circumstance. During this time, Saul had a second vision about a man named Ananias, who would come and lay his hands upon Saul, and he would receive his sight back. Ananias obeyed the Lord and went to Saul. Saul not only regained his physical sight but was also baptized, received the Holy Spirit, and became known as Paul.

After he was strengthened by food, Paul went into the synagogues and proclaimed Jesus as the Son of God. You can imagine the impact of that proclamation on those whom Paul had been persecuting! Paul did not change his view about Christians; he changed his view about God.

Paul now saw people the way God saw them. God created them all, and He loved them all. In God's view, everyone is someone special. Christ died for ALL people because He has no prejudice, bias, or favoritism. We are all equal in His sight. No one is inferior—and no one can make you feel inferior without your permission!

You can read about the rest of Paul's incredible experiences in

Acts 9:1-28, 31 (NASB). In 1 Corinthians 15:8-10 (NASB), he gives testimony to the grace of God in his life,

> *And last of all, as to one untimely born, He (Jesus) appeared to me also. For I am the least of the apostles, and not fit to be called an apostle, because I persecuted the church of God. But, by the grace of God I am what I am, and His grace toward me did not prove vain, but I labored even more than all of them, yet not I, but the grace of God within me.*

Paul further explains his new outlook on life,

> *But whatever things were gain for me, those things I have counted as loss for the sake of Christ. More than that, I count all things to be loss in view of the surpassing value of knowing Christ Jesus my Lord, whom I have suffered the loss of all things, and count them as rubbish so that I may gain Christ, and may be found in Him, not having a righteousness of my own derived from the Law, but that which is through faith in Christ, the righteousness which comes from God on the basis of faith, that I may know Him and the power of His resurrection and the fellowship of His sufferings, being conformed to His death; in order that I may attain to the resurrection from the dead* (Philippians 3:7-11 NASB).

Paul states in Galatians 3:28 (NASB): "There is neither Jew nor Greek, there is neither slave nor free man, there is neither male nor female; for you are all one in Christ Jesus." In these verses, he emphasizes that there is no race, beliefs, social status, or anything else that makes anyone superior OR inferior to anyone else.

God has created mankind in a vast diversity of cultures and races all over this world. By realizing this truth from God, you can begin to dismantle your own prejudices about any issue or individual and truly appreciate the unique gifts and abilities of your fellowmen.

If it can happen to Oskar Schindler and the Apostle Paul, it can happen to you. It is the beginning of peace and reconciliation when you realize you were blind, but now you see!

FOR PERSONAL REFLECTION AND DISCUSSION

- What do you think was Paul's greatest gift?
- How is Paul's persecution of Christians relevant to Christian persecution today?
- Do you have a favorite verse from Paul's epistles? Which one and why?

22

God Can Heal My Shame

A phenomenon called Post Traumatic Stress Disorder (PTSD) is becoming more widely known among our military personnel, both those stationed abroad and those veterans who have returned home. According to Wikipedia, PTSD is a form of mental illness involving exposure to different types of trauma that are frightening, many times overwhelming. It causes a lot of mental and emotional distress to the sufferer.

However, in a broader sense, PTSD, in varying levels of severity, can also happen to victims of child abuse, sexual abuse, date rape, sex trafficking, etc. Many times, healing from PTSD can be accomplished by counseling and other measures. However, with sexual abuse, the memories are challenging to heal, especially the betrayal aspect of the abuser. Deep, life-long scars can remain.

One of my favorite scriptures is from Isaiah 61:1-3 (NASB).

The Spirit of the Lord God is upon me, because the Lord has anointed Me to bring good news to the afflicted; He has sent Me to bind up the brokenhearted; to proclaim liberty to captives and freedom to prisoners . . . to grant those who mourn in Zion, giving them a garland instead of ashes, the oil of gladness instead of mourning, the mantle of praise instead of a spirit of fainting, so they will be called oaks of righteousness, the planting of the Lord, that He may be glorified.

For born-again believers, this promise of God holds the key to healing and restoration of sexual purity. God gives you beauty (garland) for ashes as He restores your sexual well-being and heals your memories of the past. He gives you His joy that becomes your strength. He removes the shame and faintness of heart and gives you a mantle of praise and thanksgiving because He has not forsaken you! God gives you His vision of you once again as a spiritual virgin in His sight!

I know a woman who suffered sexual abuse from a family member during her teens, both physically and verbally. In her senior year of college, she left home and became promiscuous because of her non-existent self-esteem. She saw herself as damaged goods and believed that no man could love her or even want to be with her. She became a type of prodigal son figure in wild living, having several affairs with married men.

At age 25, she met and married a man she knew from her workplace, mainly because he asked for her hand in marriage. They lived the white picket fence stereotype marriage as married singles (married in name only). When their first child came along, the tension of the mismatched pair became so great that the husband left her for another woman. Two days after his announcement, an office friend led her to salvation by sharing the four spiritual laws and a book on how a young Catholic could accept Christ. She sat down and read the book and started to talk to the Lord in prayer on her living room sofa. She had been born again!

A divorce did ensue, but she and her ex-husband have maintained an amicable relationship even to this day. After she walked with God for 12 years, He led her into the process of healing her sexual abuse memories through a Christian therapist, which was a three-year process. Halfway through the therapy, her abuser died. She was able to forgive her abuser, even though no remorse was shown to her for the wrongful actions.

Her healing continued, and her spiritual virginity was restored to her by the Lord. He brought a Christian man to become her new husband! The Lord has given her this special man to love and cherish her for the rest of her life. She learned that sexual abuse was not the unforgivable sin, and she could forgive the abuser as her heavenly Father had forgiven her.

The scars of her spiritual wounds became a gift to understand and minister to others with the grace that she had been given by God. She is a living testimony of the power of the resurrected Jesus to heal her life as well as change the lives of others. By the way, that woman is me!

My second husband, Peter, and I have been married for more than 26 years! Jesus is the center of our marriage, forming a three-strand cord that cannot be easily broken. The impossible dream evolved into being able to love three stepchildren as well as my son and six incredibly awesome grandchildren, ranging in ages from twenty-one to ten.

My husband and I are happily retired and have been given a vision by God to plant a Christian church in Lancaster County, Pennsylvania. Everything that happens to us works together for good for those who love God, to those who are called according to His purpose (Romans 8:28 NASB).

This same God is your Father in heaven, and He wants to change your life as well. He is more than able to do it and is waiting for you to ask Him. What do you have to lose? You have everything to gain! As the old hymn states, "Blessings all mine and ten thousand besides! Great is Thy Faithfulness, Lord, unto me!"

FOR PERSONAL REFLECTION AND DISCUSSION

- How would sexual abuse make a woman feel shame?
- What kinds of things make people feel shame?
- If you have felt shame, how has God helped you overcome it?

23

The Question Is—Where?

A good friend of mine and his wife came to my house for dinner. He was asking me about my faith in the face of my cancer and Stage 5 kidney disease. He sensed I had no anxiety about my situation. So I shared with him that my peace came from my total trust in God. He asked me if I believed in life after death, and when I told him I definitely did, he confessed he was not sure. He asked if I read my Bible every day, and I told him that I did and that the Bible makes it very clear. He asked me to share some scripture he could read about it. So I sent him to Luke 16. We're having lunch soon, and I'm praying he will come to know the Lord as his Savior.

The story in Luke 16 is the most definitive story in the Bible that speaks to the existence of life after death. Jesus is telling the story (not a parable because it mentions a man by name) about a rich man and a beggar named Lazarus. They both die and Lazarus was carried to Abraham's side in heaven. The rich man was buried and goes to hades (hell). From hell, the rich man can see Lazarus and Abraham. (The worst thing about hell may be seeing heaven.)

The rich man asked Abraham to send Lazarus to put water on his tongue because he was in agony in the fire. Abraham replied that it could not be done. The rich man then asked Abraham to send Lazarus back to tell his brothers, so they wouldn't go to hell. Abraham told him he couldn't do that either. The rich man replied, "If someone from the dead (Lazarus) goes to them, they will repent." Then Abraham told the rich man they won't believe even if someone rises from the dead.

So it's pretty clear from this story that once you're there—heaven or hell—there isn't anything that can be done about it. This fact makes it even more critical to determine now where you're going to spend eternity. Don't put off that decision because none of us is guaranteed tomorrow.

One irony is that Jesus really did raise a man named Lazarus from the dead. It is pretty clear from this story (that Jesus Himself told) that there is life after death—both a heaven and a hell. Based on these descriptions, let me see—yes, I think I'll choose heaven and you should too! Christ's death is your guarantee of paradise. Believe in the Lord Jesus Christ, and you will be saved. You alone make the decision whether to follow Jesus Christ and be born again, or reject Him and wind up with the rich man for eternity.

Quite a few people do not believe in life after death. Of the top five major world religions, only Christianity and Islam preach life after death. There are many differences between these two religions on that concept. Is the game over when you die? Is that all there is to look forward to? Do you grab for all the gusto and eat, drink, and be merry before your time runs out? These are very real and sobering questions everyone must answer for themselves.

Every person is created by God and given a body, a mind, and a spirit (soul), as well as the gift of free will. Some of us use these components wisely, and some of us don't. Some of our decisions shorten our lifespans, and some can add more time to our lifespans. But in the end, we all die and cease earthly living. None of us gets out of this world alive!

King Solomon, son of King David, lamented that:

There is an evil in all that is done under the sun, that there is one fate for all men. Furthermore, the hearts of the sons of men are full of evil and insanity is in their hearts throughout their lives. Afterwards, they go to the dead (Ecclesiastes 9:3).

Not a very hopeful viewpoint! Yet, in Psalm 139:8, the psalmist writes, "If I ascend to heaven, You are there; if I make my bed in Sheol (hell), behold You are there!" There was some concept of heaven and hell, but it was somewhat vague.

In God's perfect timing and wisdom, He sent His only Son, Jesus Christ, into the world as a human baby, conceived by the Holy Spirit and the Virgin Mary. As original sin was passed down through Adam, Jesus was the only sinless person who has ever lived. Jesus became the ultimate sacrifice for sin with His death on the cross. He opened the gates of heaven to all who would believe in Him.

During Jesus' public ministry, He often spoke about His Father in heaven and the Kingdom of Heaven. He explained the concept of being born again to Nicodemus.

For God so loved the world that He gave His only begotten Son, that whoever believes in Him shall not perish, but have eternal life (John 3:16).

When His good friend Lazarus died, Jesus told Martha that He

Is the Resurrection and the life, he who believes in Me will live even if he dies, and everyone who lives and believes in Me will never die (John 11:25-26).

Jesus reassured His disciples before He was crucified that they should not let their hearts be troubled, but to believe in God and believe in Jesus, because

In My Father's house are many mansions; if it were not so, I would have told you; for I go to prepare a place for you. If I go and prepare a place for you, I will come again and receive you to Myself, that where I am, there you may be also (John 14:1-3).

Two days before He was crucified, Jesus told the parable of the sheep (righteous) and the goats (evil), and their respective deeds toward those people in need. The goats would be sent into eternal punishment, and the sheep would enter eternal life with God (Matthew 25:31-46). While He was dying on the cross between the two thieves, the one thief asked Jesus to remember him when He came in His kingdom, and Jesus replied, "Truly I say to you, today you will be with Me in Paradise" (Luke 23:42-43).

In the Apostle Paul's testimony before Felix the Governor, Paul acknowledged he was a follower of Christ, a Christian, and he had "a hope in God, which these men cherish themselves, that there shall certainly be a resurrection of both the righteous and the wicked" (Acts 24:15).

Romans chapters 5-8 teach the concepts of sin and death and Christ's redemption of mankind by His ultimate sacrifice on the cross. The Book of Revelation, written by the Apostle John and the last book of the New Testament, describes the last days of the earth and Jesus' return to earth to bring forth justice for all and take His church home to heaven as His Bride for all eternity.

We're all going to live for eternity—the only question is where. The rich man and Lazarus tell the story. I choose heaven. And you have to choose too. The time for choosing is now because once we're dead, the choosing time is over. God longs for you to choose Him. Not choosing is a choice for hell. Accepting Christ as your Lord and Savior is the choice that ensures heaven. I want you to know that God wants you in heaven for eternity. He's already proven He would rather die than live without you. The choice is yours, my friend.

FOR PERSONAL REFLECTION AND DISCUSSION

- Do you believe in life after death? Why, why not?
- What did the thief on the cross think about life after death?
- Why did Jesus grant the thief's wish?

24

He Never Leaves

Have you ever witnessed a small child being dropped off at nursery school who cried and begged their mother not to leave them? I've seen it in my own family as a grandparent when Mom drops them off at my house. It is scary for them. They feel abandoned and insecure, and they're afraid Mom won't come back for them. Young kids grow attached very quickly, and it can be traumatic for them when they sense a loss of security. And perhaps it hurts Mom the most to hear their child cry, "Mommy, don't leave me."

But sometimes what parents must do is for the child's own good. I remember a story about a father who had to take his child to the emergency room with a broken arm. After they x-rayed his arm, the doctor told the father it was a bad break, and they needed to reset the arm before putting it in a cast. It would be a painful process.

During the pain, the boy cried out to his father, "Make them stop, Daddy!" He repeated that request a few times and then asked, "Daddy, why won't you make them stop?" It tore the father's heart apart. Yet the father knew it was for his son's own good. But the father never left him.

Our God is like that. Sometimes He lets things happen because He knows in the long term, it's for our own good. But He never leaves us.

Nowadays, with everything going on in the world—persecution, pestilence, political takeovers, and divisiveness—it's easy to take comfort in the familiar description, "Bad things happening to good people." This gives people an excuse to turn off God in their lives. God gets blamed for allowing such unthinkable things to happen all the time. He is letting us down because bad things happen. But the truth is that good and bad things happen to all people!

The two basic ingredients of living in this world are the elements of good and evil. For example, prosperity, health, and peace are deemed good while poverty, sickness, and war are considered to be evil. But the thread that runs through all of humanity is the presence of free will—the ability to be good and do well versus the ability to be evil and do terrible things. We are truly blessed not to be puppets on a string but can choose what we want in any given situation.

It all began in Genesis 1:1-2:26 when the universe was created along with the birds, mammals, fish, and man and woman. God looked down at His creation and saw it was very good. The Garden of Eden was Paradise, the perfect beginning to a happy hereafter. God walked with Adam and Eve in the cool of the evening and shared fellowship with them together every day. They were naked and unashamed. Everything was cool!

But in Genesis 3:1-7, the serpent, representing evil, slithered into the Garden and confronted the innocent Eve. Through a series of rationalizations, he tempted her and smooth-talked her into eating the fruit of the forbidden tree. The party was over! Sin had entered the world, and we inherited a sinful nature.

You would think the first sin was not so bad to deserve the consequences God meted out. But God is holy and righteous, and He requires and expects obedience to His commands. The serpent was doomed to crawl on its belly forever, Eve would endure great pain during childbirth, and Adam had to do hard physical labor in planting crops all the days of his life. Their oldest son, Cain, killed his brother Abel over jealousy of God's favor.

Sin had taken hold of the earth. Sin became a contender for our free will to twist, distort, and deny God's goodness in His creation. We became part of the human condition; each of us is sentenced to endure hardships, suffering, and death and return to dust because of Adam's sin.

Today there seems to be a life-and-death struggle worldwide between good and evil for dominion in global power and control in unimaginable dimensions.

Why is there suffering and chaos? Why is there so much division over race, gender, and wealth? Why are there hatred and deception and lust for power and glory? Because there is sin! All people bear the brunt of these evil things, even though they have not necessarily done anything wrong.

Evil drives distraught, hurting people with tragic circumstances who are desperate to have things be right again. They lash out in evil ways in an attempt to regain control of their lives and make their own utopias. But, the eternal promise of God is that in heaven, there will be no more night, no more pain, no more tears again (Revelation 21:4).

God wants us to look beyond the circumstances of our life. He knows sin reigns on this earth, and bad things happen to all people. And He has made provision for us to endure. Paul advises us not to be conformed to this world, but

To be transformed by the renewing of your mind, so that you may prove what the will of God is, that which is good and acceptable and perfect (Romans 12:2).

We are to:

Fix our eyes on Jesus, the Author and Perfector of our faith, who for the joy set before Him endured the cross, despising the shame, and has sat down at the right hand of the throne of God (Hebrews 12:2).

If God is for us, who can be against us? Paul states in Romans 8:38-39,

I am convinced that neither death, nor life, nor angels, nor principalities, nor things present, nor things to come, nor powers, nor height, nor depth, nor any other created thing will be able to separate us from the love of God, which is in Christ Jesus our Lord.

God's love and justice are unparalleled to anything on earth. Evil is prevalent everywhere—as Peter warns us in 1 Peter 5:8, "Be of sober spirit, be on the alert. Our adversary, the devil prowls around like a roaring lion, seeking someone to devour." We live in a sinful world with sin all around us. But by God's grace, we can overcome any circumstance in our lives.

Life happens to each one of us. We are human beings, living in a finite world that will end one day when Jesus returns to the earth once more. Then, every wrong shall be righted, every sinful act revealed and punished, and the people of God will enjoy the Garden of Eden with God once more for eternity!

God never promised us a life without pain or struggle or hardship. He just promised He would be there with us, and we would never have to go through it alone. I want you to know that like the father of the boy with the broken arm, He never leaves our side. So whatever circumstance you're going through, you can be sure God is right there with you.

Sure, bad things happen. But Jesus said, "In this world you will have trouble. But take heart! I have overcome the world" (John 16:33). Because He overcame, we can too! Our perspective is eternal, not temporal. Remember, "God works all things together for the good for those who love God."

FOR PERSONAL REFLECTION AND DISCUSSION

- Has there been a time when you did not do what your child asked you to do? How did it make you feel?
- Describe a time in your life when you felt God's presence.

25

The Mountain or the Molehill?

There have been times in my life, and probably yours, where we did or said something we thought was trivial or non-offensive, but others thought it was a big deal or offensive. Our idea of a big deal is not always what others might think of as a big deal. What seems like a mountain to us is just a molehill for others. And vice versa, what may seem like a molehill to us might be a mountain for someone else. So how does God view our sins—are they mountains or molehills?

Certainly, by human reasoning, some actions appear more egregious than others. Going five miles an hour over the posted speed limit is not as bad as premeditated murder. In the Catholic faith, sins are ranked from lesser venial sins up to biggie, mortal sins, based on the perceived severity of the sinful act. This practice would seem to make sense from a human viewpoint.

Many people view the Ten Commandments as God's gold standard for measuring our transgressions. Nonetheless, is honoring your parents or occasionally telling a white lie seems less egregious than stealing.

But did you know we don't become sinners when we commit our first sin? We commit our first sin because we are born sinners, which is called inheriting original sin. This tendency is part of our human nature, and we inherited that human, sinful nature from Adam and Eve. You don't have to teach or coax your children to lie because they come by it naturally.

When I saw my little daughter one day with powdered sugar all over her face and asked her, "Did you eat the donut?" her immediate answer was no. Nobody taught her to lie; she just knew how to lie because it was part of her human nature. By her answer, she indicated she knew the lie was in her best interest and did it anyway.

This fatal flaw in our human nature is that it is based on our access to free will given to us by God. Like Adam and Eve, we have a choice to make in any situation, and we too have knowledge of the tree of good and evil, just like they did in the Garden of Eden. God acknowledges that "Our thoughts are not His thoughts, and our ways are not His ways" (Isaiah 55:8). So, before we can say our sins aren't that bad, we should know and understand what God thinks about our sins.

First, God hates all sin because it goes against His character of holiness and righteousness. God says that all have all sinned and fallen short of His glory (Romans 3:23). Few of us would disagree with this statement. We all have an innate sense that we have done something wrong in our lives that even we would categorize as sin.

But God goes on to state that, "The wages of sin is death" (Romans 6:23). So, from God's perspective, all sin deserves the death penalty—mortal or venial, big or little. No matter how you try to categorize your sin, rationalize your sin, or see your sin, God sees all sin as punishable by death. Sin separates us from God, which means we are separated from the ultimate source of life, and the result is death.

You might say, "Wait just a minute! All sin is punishable by death? Isn't that a bit drastic and harsh and overreacting? I don't consider myself to be a bad person! I'm basically a righteous person. How can God say that?" Our holy God says He sees all our righteousness as filthy rags (Isaiah 64:6). In Romans 3:10, Paul confirms that "None are righteous, not even one!" So, when you say, "My sins aren't that bad," God says, "Oh yes, they are!" And that is NOT good news!

But the good news is God has made divine provision for your

sins. He sent His Son, Jesus Christ, to die on the cross to pay the debt for your sin! Because of what Jesus did, God offers forgiveness and salvation as a gift to all who accept Christ as their Savior.

But it is even bigger than that. Consider the spider and the spider web. The web represents our sins. And God can forgive those. But the real problem is not the web—it's the spider. If you tear down a spider web, the spider will just make another one. So, the problem is not the web—it's the spider. The problem is us! We are sin-making machines just like the spider is a web-making machine. But God not only forgives our sins, He forgives us. He makes provision for His Holy Spirit to indwell us and give us a new life. He replaces the spider's life with His life!

In my mind's eye, I can envision a courtroom scene on Judgment Day. Satan is the prosecuting attorney, and he has spent hours presenting the evidence of every one of my sins. I'm sitting at the defense table with Jesus as my defense attorney. I'm embarrassed and ashamed by all these accusations, and, worst of all, I know all the accusations are true. I had done everything Satan was accusing me of doing.

I'm guilty by any and every measure, beyond any shadow of a doubt. Satan concludes his closing arguments by saying, "Your Honor, the prosecution is seeking the death penalty in this case. The prosecution rests."

Jesus then stands to address the court. He says, "Your Honor (God), everything the prosecution has said about my client is true. But as you know, My death on the cross has already paid the penalty for those sins. The death penalty the prosecution is seeking has already taken place by My death. And my client, Mr. White, accepted My death and resurrection as the punishment for those sins. He accepted Me as his Lord and Savior many years ago. Therefore, Your Honor, we believe the defendant is not guilty, and the defense rests!" God doesn't take two seconds to say, "Case dismissed. Mr. White, you are free to go!"

Both your sins and my sins are that bad! We all need a Savior. It is so much better to know your sins are forgiven than to assume your sins just aren't that bad. You will feel differently, act differently, and create better results for yourself that will better meet your needs over time! I want you to know God forgives your sins, and He forgives you!

FOR PERSONAL REFLECTION AND DISCUSSION

- Do you tend to categorize sins as big or small? Why, why not?
- Do you judge others because they sin differently? Why, why not?
- Why do people tend to think their sins are small?

26

God Answers Every Prayer

The concept of prayer today seems to be a multi-part exercise of telling God what you want from Him. How frustrating it is when you pray and nothing happens, or you get what you didn't ask for instead! So, if there is seemingly no consistency in asking God for things and not receiving them, why should you pray?

First of all, God is NOT a genie in a lamp where you get three wishes granted if you rub the lamp! God is NOT an ATM machine, dispensing money or rewards or tips on the winning horses at your favorite racetrack! God is NOT your valet or manservant to be ordered around and disdained if He doesn't perform to your satisfaction daily. God is NOT Santa Claus, the Easter Bunny, or the Tooth Fairy. God doesn't get all mushy if you try to manipulate Him by sending compliments or making promises you will never keep. He is Almighty God!

So, what is prayer? Simply put, prayer is communication between you and God. Many churches have formal, written prayers that are said during church services. But a lot of people don't know how to talk to God in their own words. The good news is you don't have to be eloquent or long-winded or even spiritual when you pray. My most often-used prayer is "Help!"—not tremendously spiritual but very effective!

Jesus taught His disciples about prayer in Matthew 6:5-13 (NASB). He showed them an example of how not to pray: "When you pray, don't be like the hypocrites, for they love to stand and pray in the synagogues and on the street corner so they will be seen

107

by men. Truly I say to you, they have their reward in full" (Matthew 6:5 NASB). That is not the best way to pray because those folks do it for show and are not earnestly seeking God.

God's directions are to "go into your inner closet, close the door and pray to your Father in secret, and your Father who sees what is done in secret will reward you." It's like Aunt Clara in the movie *War Room*. She went into her prayer closet every day and had lists of people to pray for taped onto her closet wall!

But wait, there's more! God continues with His instructions:

> *And when you are praying, do not use meaningless repetition as the Gentiles do, for they suppose that they will be heard for their many words. So, do not be like them; for your Father knows what you need before you ask Him* (Matthew 6:7-8 NASB).

Jesus then taught His disciples the Lord's Prayer (Matthew 6:9-13 NASB). He constructed it in this order: 1) addressing God as our Father in heaven as the recipient of this prayer; 2) honoring the sanctity of God's name; 3) acknowledging His authority over heaven and earth for His will to be done. The actual request doesn't start until this part of the prayer. The prayer request(s) come after the acknowledgment of His holiness. The petitions are about daily needs: actual food to eat, grace to forgive others as He has forgiven us, helping us to avoid temptation, and delivering us from evil (physically, mentally, and spiritually).

Referring back to the beginning of this chapter, praying is asking God for something—not demanding that He does what you have been praying for. In Matthew 7:7-11 (NASB), Jesus teaches us to be active in our prayers—

> *Ask, and it will be given to you; seek and you will find; knock, and the door will be opened to you. For everyone who asks, receives, and he who seeks, finds and to him who knocks, it will be opened.*

He continues,

Or what man is there among you who, when his son asks for a loaf, will give him a stone? Or if he asks for a fish, will give him a snake? If you, being evil, know how to give good gifts to your children, how much more will your Father who is in heaven give what is good to those who ask Him?

The truth of prayer is that God always answers EVERY prayer directed to Him. His answer may be yes, no, or not now. Being your heavenly Father and knowing all things, God will not give you something that is wrong, selfish, or harmful! He loves you too much to accommodate your whims or wants. Just as your parents protected you from danger when you were growing up, God will protect you from harming yourself through making wrong choices when you ask for His input.

The Holy Spirit is a Counselor about the laws and ways of God the Father. You can offer up a prayer through Jesus, Who sits at the right hand of the Father and intercedes for us as well. God never sleeps, never puts you on hold or uses an answering machine because He is never too busy to hear and answer your prayer!

There is an old saying that there are no atheists in foxholes in the heat of battle in a war. Stories have been written and plays produced that focus on that foxhole promise or vow/oath to do something for God if they survive that situation. Later, the soldier regrets that vow was made and doesn't know how to get out of it. You cannot bargain with God in a give-and-take atmosphere—God knows what you need before you ask Him!

He doesn't intervene in the prayer request until He is asked. He has given us all free will, and we need to choose to go to Him in prayer. He will not force us to do that. We must choose to come before Him (without one plea, but that Jesus' blood was shed for me), and He bids us to come to Him for help in the very present trouble. That's how it works!

There are dynamic results for a prayer warrior who prays in love for other people's needs or situations. In 1 Peter 4:8 (NASB), Peter says that we should keep fervent in our love for one another because love covers a multitude of sins. Fervent prayer can turn a sinner from the error of his ways, will save the sinner's soul from death, and will cover a multitude of sins. (James 5:20 NASB).

So, there you have it. Try to pray with this mindset according to God's directive and understand His ways. Bet you will get more prayers answered!

FOR PERSONAL REFLECTION AND DISCUSSION

- What different types of prayers have you prayed?
- Has God answered a prayer in your life? Describe.
- Why is prayer important to you?

27

Christ Is My Life

So many miraculous things abound in this world! Its preservation in perfect physical order is one. So is the miracle of birth—creating a new human life and bringing it into the world. The physiology of the human body and how every part supports each other is utterly amazing! We often take these miracles for granted and don't appreciate the divine Creator who called everything into being.

Many of us are overwhelmed with everyday life—situations, decisions, surprises, and challenges—not only for ourselves but for our spouses, children, parents, neighbors, and colleagues. We pretty well set up our own individual systems on how to deal with everything in our lives. So, when something unexpected happens, we deal with it and go back about our schedules as we had planned.

Before I was born again, I lived my life my way, and nothing seemed to go right. My sins kept forever piling up with no end in sight. One afternoon in early May 1977, I asked God into my life and experienced my spiritual rebirth in Christ. It was the first of many miracles in my new life as His child!

When we get saved (born again), it changes everything. There is the excitement of being free of sin because we are forgiven, and God's overwhelming love gives us spiritual goosebumps! But when we settle back down to everyday life, somehow, much of that excitement fades. We inevitably tend to revert to our comfortable habits (and sins), and our lives continue as usual.

This type of behavior must certainly disappoint God. When we ask God to be the Lord of our lives, we are making a covenant (sacred commitment) with Him. We lay down our plans for our lives and pick up His cross and His plans for our lives. This covenant with God is as binding and permanent as a marriage covenant where the bride and groom become one flesh before God. If a groom leaves the wedding reception and goes drinking all night, or a bride spends the night with an old boyfriend, then the marriage would appear not to be based on a covenant but on convenience.

Paul the Apostle has a lot to say about this new life with God. In Galatians 2:20 (NASB), he writes,

> *I have been crucified with Christ; and it is no longer I who live, but Christ lives in me; and the life which I now live in the flesh I live by faith in the Son of God, who loved me and gave Himself up for me.*

Paul further states, "now those who belong to Christ Jesus have crucified the flesh with its passions and desires" (Galatians 5:24 NASB). That doesn't mean you lose all of your passions and desires—it means you offer them to God's lordship in your life. If there are idols in your life like sports, celebrities, travel, or entertainment, you must lay them aside. If there are sinful behaviors like gossiping, coveting, stealing, cheating on your spouse, or substance abuse, you must lay them down before the Lord and give them up to Him for keeps! There is nothing wrong with having good activities in your life, but when they become idols and replace God in your life, they become wrong and sinful.

Just because you have been forgiven of all of your past sins, the decision to follow Christ does not give you license to conduct yourself as business as usual. Salvation is not a signed piece of paper you can put on a shelf or in a safety deposit box and forget about it. God's love and salvation create a daily, dynamic relationship that draws you into His love and mercies as well as His faithfulness and righteousness.

God's grace in saving us through faith is not a license to continue to do whatever we want. Sin is still sin, and it is not what God wants for you. In our experience, the people who accept Christ as their Savior change their behavior because they *want* to—not because they *have* to. It is out of thankfulness that they change their lives. So, while anyone can try to go on sinning boldly, they usually don't because God's love intervenes in their hearts.

Let's talk a bit more about changes in your life—thinking patterns, new behaviors, etc. If you were chugging beer all night and coming home drunk before you became a Christian, people would definitely take notice if you suddenly are limiting your drinking with the guys and coming home sober. If you were the town gossip and told everything about everybody to everybody else, people would notice if you stopped doing that and remained quiet and peaceful. If you regularly bet on the horses and lost money all the time, going into significant debt, people would notice if you stopped gambling.

Note the major problem here is out-of-control compulsion. Abandoning a sinful life and accepting the Christian lifestyle sets an example for everyone to notice and wonder how you turned your life around (which is your testimony). They will see they too can change their lives by accepting God's forgiveness for their sins because you set the example.

This is not to say you will never sin again because you will. But when you sin or start to fall back into old sinful ways, know that you can be forgiven and restored by God when you confess your sins to Him (1 John 1:9 NASB). You can be real with God all the time as a Christian! He forgives you and does not remember those sins anymore!

So, as Jesus said to the woman caught in adultery after all of her accusers left her, "Woman, where are they? Did no one condemn you?" She said, "No one, Lord." And Jesus said, "I don't condemn you either. Go from here and sin no more" (John 8:3-11 NASB). Likewise, God will give you all the help you need to overcome sin in your life. Hallelujah!

FOR PERSONAL REFLECTION AND DISCUSSION

- Have you kept on sinning after salvation? Why do you think that is?
- What does it mean to you to be crucified with Christ?
- How has your life been a witness to others?

28

Knowing God's Voice

In Chapter 26, the focus was on prayer: how God hears and answers every one of them in His perfect timing and wisdom; and how to pray, using the Lord's prayer as an example. However, many scriptures in the Bible tell how God spoke to His people through a direct voice, dreams and visions, angelic visitations, etc. Listed below are some examples to explore:

Old Testament references
- Genesis 3:1-24 - Adam and Eve in Garden of Eden
- Genesis 15:1-21—the Abrahamic Covenant with God
- Genesis 18:1-15—three strangers' prophecy of the birth of Isaac, Abraham's biological son
- 1 Sam 3:2-10—Samuel as a boy
- I Kings 19:11-13—Elijah in the cave at Horeb
- Isaiah 6:8—Isaiah's vision in the Temple
- Jonah 1:1-2—Jonah's instructions to go to Nineveh
- All the major and minor prophets

New Testament references
- Matthew 1:18-25—Joseph told by an angel to take Mary as his wife
- Matthews 2:8-12—Magi find Baby Jesus and warned by God not to tell Herod
- Matthew 2:13,19,21-23—Joseph to take Mary and Jesus to Egypt, Joseph to bring the family back to Israel, Joseph to take family and settle in Nazareth

- Matthew 17:1-8—Transfiguration of Jesus
- Mark 1:9-11—Baptism of Jesus
- Acts 9:1-7; 10-19—Paul's encounter with Jesus and vision of Ananias to visit Paul and heal his physical blindness
- Revelation—whole book

But there are also times when God speaks a word to us as individuals when we are not praying. I have experienced this in different ways in my walk with the Lord. In the midst of my day, the Lord can place a person—a family member, a friend, a stranger—on my heart and urge me to lift that one up in prayer. Later, I find out that the person that I prayed for had encountered some danger or accident that he/she had been in the midst of and was miraculously rescued from it.

Another time, the Lord would draw me to a particular passage of Scripture. Later in the day, I would encounter someone in need of encouragement and share the passage that perfectly met their need. Occasionally, when I am alone, I have heard a voice calling my name when no one is there and realize that it is the Lord who is speaking it.

In John 10:1-15, Jesus describes Himself as the Good Shepherd and declares that His sheep know His voice. They will not follow the voice(s) of strangers but only the voice of the Shepherd. As each one of us inwardly digests God's Word and responds to the promptings of the Holy Spirit, we too will learn to recognize the voice of the Shepherd.

Joyce:
Peter and I met in the National Christian Choir in 1985. On the Choir's 10th anniversary in 1994, we planned a special reunion, and all former and current members were invited. Peter had left the Choir in 1988 because of a hectic travel schedule with his newly formed company.

When he received the invitation, he ignored it—his wife had

116

died from cancer in October 1993, and his priorities were else-where. A week before the reunion, the Lord spoke to him that he must attend! In a panic, he called the Choir office, thinking he had missed it. In reality, the reunion was that coming weekend!

I had known Peter as a friend when he first joined the Choir, but I had no contact with him for six years. We met again at the re-union and were instantly drawn to each other. We got engaged later that spring and were married the day after Thanksgiving. Obviously, God had a plan for our lives together!

In my 26-year marriage to Peter, many times we have been like-minded—totally in sync with each other. At those times, he would start a sentence, and I would finish it or vice versa because we were of one mind—spouses in sync. This doesn't happen every day, but it is a joy when it does happen!

Steve:

I became a Christian in 1969, and while I've never heard God's audible voice, He speaks to me all the time. I've been married to Sherrie now for 36 years, and I know her very well. The same is true of God when you've known God for more than 50 years as I have. I know how Sherrie will respond in certain situations because I know how she will feel in them. I know her likes and dislikes. She doesn't always need to speak for me to know what she's thinking or what she wants me to do.

The same is true with God. I just know His nature, His char-acter, what pleases Him, and how He has responded previously. The Holy Spirit just gives me the slightest nudge, and I'll know what to do or say.

My greatest experiences of God speaking to me usually come in my dreams, not deep dreams, but that early morning time when you wake-up but don't get up; and you're in a dream-like state of la-la land. That's when God usually gives me the bigger things. One night I had been reading in John 15:5 about the vine and the branches, and I remember thinking, *I wonder what that would feel like?* During the night in a dream God gave me, I wondered what it would feel like. I was absolutely blown away.

More recently in writing this book, Joyce and I had finished a review session with our agent Keith. He did not like the premise of our book and encouraged us to rewrite it from a different perspective. I have to admit it was a little deflating, but I took his words as from God and began thinking of how to rewrite the manuscript. The next morning while in my la-la land, God gave me the new title (and subtitle), an entirely new introduction, and a new theme for the book. When I got up, I rewrote the introduction in about ten minutes.

Maybe God speaks to you differently, but this is how He most often speaks to me. If he can speak to Balaam (Numbers 22:22) through a donkey, I suppose He can speak to you any way He wants to. The point is that God speaks. And the longer you know Him, the closer your relationship with Him, the clearer His voice will become to you.

Joyce:

I genuinely believe that each of God's children can experience this same like-mindedness in their individual relationship with Him. One amazing example is how the Lord encouraged both Steve and me to write this book!

Steve and I graduated from the same little high school in Sandy Spring, Maryland—the Class of '65! We didn't know each other at that time because of our different interests. After graduation, we went our separate ways.

In the summer of 2019, I found Steve on Facebook and became his friend. He and his wife live in Atlanta, Georgia, and Peter and I live in Gordonville, Pennsylvania.

On Facebook, I learned that he had written and published two books in 2012. In a Facebook post, he encouraged me to read both of his books and give him feedback. I genuinely enjoyed that and casually asked when he was going to write his next book. His response was to ask me to be his co-author on this book! Evidently, the Lord was at work in both of our lives 55 years after graduation!

As we began to organize the concept of the book, the Lord gave each of us different topics to develop. As I have never written a book before, I thought I would have a long learning curve. When deciding what to write on a specific topic, the Lord would give me ideas and scriptures with examples in my dreams. Afterward, I would get up and write it up. Amazing!

The most incredible result was that we were able to use all of our original material as we re-thought and re-wrote the manuscript. This new manuscript is truly now His book, not our book.

Both Steve and I can testify to the goodness and faithfulness of our God when we are in sync with Him and His plan for each of our lives. Wonder what God will do next? Perhaps He will speak to you through this book—that would be just like Him! Hallelujah!

FOR PERSONAL REFLECTION AND DISCUSSION

- Do you have a favorite Bible verse about God speaking? Why?
- Why do you think God speaks to people? To you?
- The Creator of heaven and earth knows your name and wants to speak to you. How does that make you feel?

29

God Can Relate

So many families have lost sons and daughters in war. Other families have lost children to disease, substance abuse, car accidents, or suicide. A parent wants to know, "Where was God when my child died?" Joyce remembers asking this same question when her only child died of an opioid overdose three years ago. And the answer is quite simply, "The same place He was when His Son died." God knows and understands your pain. He can relate because He too lost a Son. He had to watch His only Son—innocent, blameless, and sinless—die on a cross.

His Son suffered humiliation, mocking, beating, and ultimately crucifixion, and God didn't stop it from happening. God also had to indescribably suffer when He heard the words from His Son, "Why have You forsaken Me?" How it must have broken His heart to have to turn away from His own Son, when His Son needed Him most. His Son prayed earlier to be spared the cross. But God allowed it because He loved you and me that much.

For those of you who have lost children to war, I am reminded of Abraham Lincoln's words in a letter to a Mrs. Bixby, who had lost five sons in the Civil War.

> I pray that our Heavenly Father will assuage the anguish of your bereavement, and leave you with the solemn pride that must be yours alone, for having laid so costly a sacrifice on the altar of freedom. I am personally so sorry for your loss, and I thank you for your children's service.

But I want you to know God can relate to you. He feels your pain. He yearns to come alongside you and commiserate with you because you've both lost a child. Feel His everlasting arms embrace you in your sorrow. Lean on Him, not your own understanding. Tell Him how you feel; He understands, and more than that, He loves you.

So how could a loving God allow such horrible things to happen? The truth is God is not a puppeteer orchestrating all the events in our lives. The truth is that good and bad things happen to all people. The sun comes up each day and shines on both the good and the evil. But the one thing God has promised is no matter what we face—good or bad—He will be there with us! Jesus said, "I am with you always, even to the end of the age" (Matthew 28:20). And God said, "I will never will I leave you; never will I forsake you" (Hebrews 13:5).

God gave us free will. Adam and Eve had a choice to make in the Garden of Eden. Because they chose to disobey, we all suffer the consequences of that choice. But while we each have free will, we are not free from the consequences when we exercise that will. Many bad outcomes in life are the results of our own bad decisions, not punishment from God.

We do not have control over life's circumstances. Life seems to come at all of us at 100 mph every day, but we do have control over what we think about it. Everything that happens in our life must be viewed against the backdrop of the cross. God has settled once and for all that He loves us by sending His Son to die on the cross for our sins! We need to view all of life in that context. And more than that, He has promised to always be with us. You don't have to face any circumstance, including the death of a child, without Him. This must be our constant thought no matter what happens.

God is sovereign. Sovereignty means greatest in status, authority, and power and not controlled by outside forces. God's ways are not our ways; His thoughts are not our thoughts. (Isaiah 55:8).

God doesn't owe us any answers to our why questions. God said everything we need to know at the cross. For us now, it is just trust and obey! Paul said in Roman 8:28 that "All things work together for good for those who love God." We can trust that in any circumstance—even in the death of a loved one.

A great story in the Old Testament (Genesis 37) tells about Joseph, the youngest son of Jacob. Joseph had eleven brothers, but Jacob loved Joseph the best, and his brothers hated him for it. They plotted to kill him and threw him in a cistern (an empty dry well). Then Joseph's brother, Judah, suggested instead of killing him, they should sell him into slavery to some Midianite merchants for twenty shekels of silver. The Midianites then sold Joseph to Potiphar, the captain of the guard to the Egyptian Pharaoh.

Potiphar put Joseph in charge of his household and everything he owned. Potiphar's wife then tried to seduce Joseph, but Joseph refused her advances. She then lied and told her husband Joseph had tried to have sex with her. Potiphar threw Joseph into prison.

The prison warden put Joseph in charge of all the prisoners. Joseph remained in prison for two years. One day Joseph was summoned by Pharaoh because he had heard Joseph might be able to interpret one of his dreams. So, when Joseph interpreted Pharaoh's dream correctly, Pharaoh put Joseph in charge of all of Egypt.

When widespread famine came, Jacob sent his sons to Egypt to buy grain. When Joseph's brothers realized who Joseph was and the power Joseph held in Egypt, they were afraid and asked for forgiveness. And Joseph's reply was epic, "You intended to harm me, but God intended it for good to accomplish what is now being done, the saving of many lives" (Genesis 50:20).

When seemingly bad things happen to you, God intends it for good—even if we can't see it at the time. All things work together for good, to those who love God (Romans 8:28).

God can relate to your pain and suffering through losing a loved one—because He did too!

FOR PERSONAL REFLECTION AND DISCUSSION

- Have you ever blamed God for something bad that happened? Explain.
- What do you think God felt when His Son asked, "Why have You forsaken Me?"
- Share some bad circumstance God used for the good in your life.

30

A Sunday Reunion

As a child, I went to church with my parents and siblings when the Mass was said in Latin, and sermons focused on the material needs of the parish. My church had separate Sunday School lessons on another day. As an adult, I stopped going to church because it didn't do anything for me, even though the Mass was now in English. When I was pregnant with my son, I decided I needed to go back to church so my son could be baptized. When he was ten months old, I met the Lord and gave my life to Him as my Savior and Lord. Everything about church changed!

Many of us have memories of being dragged to church with our parents or grandparents and then to Sunday school. As we grew up, many of us decided to skip going to church on Sunday because the services were long and boring. Or if we did attend, it was out of a sense of duty. Sometimes the sermon was good, but often it was tedious, especially if the preacher spoke in monotones with no animation or emphasis shown. It was a discreet time to visit the restroom or check your phone and get through the time allotted.

Men's and women's groups tried to satisfy our spiritual needs, but many times the meetings were merely beehives of conversation and gossip and exchanging recipes or sharing about the playoffs with no mention of God or the Bible. Ultimately, we would go home without ever really meeting God there. Does any of that resonate with you? In Acts 2:1-40 (NASB), the birth of the church is detailed on the day of Pentecost.

Over 3,000 people were converted and baptized because of the sermon Peter preached! Many people weren't locals—they came from areas in Asia Minor, northern Africa, and Rome. But the miracle of Pentecost was that every person heard Peter's sermon in his/her own native language! Imagine the excitement and joy on that day. These new believers soon began to live the Christian life corporately (Acts 2:41-47 NASB).

The early Christians devoted a major part of the day to hearing the Apostles' teaching; they hung out together, they ate together, they prayed together! They all felt a sense of awe, and signs and wonders were everyday occurrences. They held everything they owned in common. Some of them began to sell their property and possessions and shared the profits among the group, caring for the needs of others.

Day by day, they did everything together with gladness and sincerity of heart. They were continually praising God and finding favor with all people, and the Lord was adding to their number daily those who were being saved! Most churches don't act that way today. Why not?

The nitty-gritty problem is Church starts with having a personal relationship with God and not a membership in a particular group. That's what Acts 2 is all about. If you don't have a personal relationship with God, i.e., been born again, you will miss the whole reason why Sunday worship services exist. Some denominations require you to attend church every week under pain of committing a sin. It becomes drudgery, especially if you are not feeling well or have an important sports event or theater tickets awaiting your return home.

Some churches offer Saturday night alternative services to free you up to accomplish these secular activities on Sunday. There is nothing wrong with fulfilling your Sunday obligation by going to Church Saturday night. Seventh Day Adventists celebrate their Sabbath/Sunday services on Saturday mornings, and that is fine.

Believe it or not, your Father in heaven, who created you and everything else in the universe, longs to have a special family time with you on Sundays (Sabbath). Church services were meant to accommodate the corporate gathering of like-minded Christians to meet with Him and enjoy their time in praise and worship and teaching.

To God, Sundays are like when a grandparent who is anxiously anticipating spending time with their children and grandchildren corporately or individually, gets to do so. Most families look forward to family reunions to celebrate one another, make amends when needed, be in awe of what a family member has done, and share their lives.

But many of us don't feel that way towards going to church for the simple reason we don't know who God is on a personal level— or have a one-on-one relationship with Him (be born again). To them, He's this distant big guy somewhere up in heaven who is stern and exacting and unreachable. The truth is God is a loving and gracious Father, who loved the world so much He sent Jesus Christ, His only Son, to earth to live as a human being and experience everything we experience.

Jesus Christ became the ultimate sacrifice for our sins and died on the cross at Calvary to atone for every sin that was ever committed. Then He rose from the dead, ascended back to His Father in heaven, and sent the Holy Spirit to live within every person who has accepted His free gift of salvation to counsel and guide us in God's Word of truth, the Bible.

Born-again Christians eagerly await corporate services each Sunday. They sing to His praise and glory, and they embrace the written prayers and are encouraged to make up their own prayers as well. They listen and inwardly digest the scripture readings and the sermon, learning more of God's Word and ways for growing into a deeper relationship with God.

The best parts are hearing the Word of God preached and taking part in the Lord's Supper and Communion. Sunday worship is a personal and sacred time that blesses everyone who comes with the knowledge God the Father will meet them there in a special way. That's an Acts 2 worship experience!

After the service, we return home or go about our day, feeling renewed, encouraged, and blessed. Sunday morning worship is the keystone to spiritual activities during the week, with home Bible studies, home group meetings, etc. God the Father gives us His amazing grace each day to help us live joyfully and not become anxious or depressed. We pray for each other, help meet the personal and practical needs of others, encourage each other, and love one another as God loves us.

The good news is you don't need a ticket to go to church, and most of the year, the weather is accommodating for your attendance. I can almost feel the adrenaline becoming stronger as Sunday/Sabbath approaches and my heavenly Father is waiting to meet me there—how about you?

FOR PERSONAL REFLECTION AND DISCUSSION

- Has going to church ever been a bummer for you? Explain.
- How is going to church most meaningful to you?
- How did not going to church affect you during the COVID-19 virus?

31

Being vs. Doing

I remember watching a video of an Olympic long-distance race called the marathon. Two runners entered the Olympic stadium after running 26 miles to finish the last two laps on the track inside. The lead runner was about 50 yards ahead of the second runner. As they approached the finish line, the lead runner collapsed on the track with a leg injury.

The runner in second place closed rapidly, but instead of running past and winning the race, he stopped and helped the injured runner to his feet. Arm-in-arm with him, he supported the injured runner to the finish line and allowed him to cross it first. It was one of the most amazing displays of sportsmanship I have ever seen!

After the race, the man asked why he had done it. His answer was, "He was clearly going to win the race. He was the best runner out here. It was just the right thing to do." It was more important to him to do the right thing and show extraordinary kindness, than to win the race. For this man, being kind came before winning! Being comes before doing.

When I was saved, I knew I had done nothing to secure my salvation. Jesus had done it all, and it was a gift from God. I had not done anything to deserve it, and I had done nothing to earn it. But after I was saved, all of a sudden, my church had a list for me of all the do's and don'ts for good Christians. As my current pastor says about his childhood church, "I grew up in a church that was against everything." So, here is just a partial list of what my church's behavior required:

Should do:
- Be baptized
- Tithe (give 10% to the church)
- Join a Sunday School class
- Sing in the choir
- Join the intercessory prayer ministry
- Share my faith with everyone
- Come to church whenever the doors were open
- Take communion

Should Not Do:
- No more drinking alcohol
- No more swearing
- No more violating any of the 10 Commandments
- No more dancing
- No more premarital sex
- No more gossiping
- No more anything FUN

In my naiveté about the Christian life, my first question was, "How many of the things on the Should Do list had been done by the thief on the cross next to Jesus?" The correct answer is NONE! He didn't have time for any Should Do list—he was dying on a cross!

Salvation equals Jesus alone + NOTHING ELSE! None of those things are required for salvation. What we do is an outgrowth of our salvation—faith and good works. As I grew in my faith, I started doing many of them, not out of obligation, but because I wanted to do them willingly and joyfully. I believe Jesus wants us to be baptized, to celebrate communion, and to support our local church. My goal in obeying Jesus by doing those things was to thank God for what He had done for me. I wanted to please Him and become more like Him.

In my experience, many of the self-appointed legalists in churches have enacted man-made rules about acceptable and unacceptable behaviors. It is always best to be sure these lists can be supported with Scripture. If something can't, then it is probably a man-made rule or tradition. No man-made rule is any better or worse than any other man-made rule. The validating measuring stick is always to fact check with God's Word!

Jesus summed up the entire law of the Old Testament with two statements: 1) Love the Lord your God with all your heart, mind, soul, and strength, and 2) Love your neighbor as yourself. That is what God's law requires of you in two simple statements. I don't need to do anything but obey them. I believe God wants me to keep the Ten Commandments, and by loving Him and my neighbor as myself those commandments will be kept. But the main thing is to just love Him and love your neighbor—that's all He asks.

It's all about the love, not the doing. Jesus cares more about who we are than what we do. The Christian life is not about performance—it is about relationship! Your relationship with God and your relationship with your neighbor is the key. So, forget the idea of a Christian 'to do' list. Just love God and your neighbor as yourself. His burden is easy and His yoke is light! (Matthew 11:29).

Maybe your church has a 'Should Do' and a 'Should Not Do' list as well, and maybe you judge people by what they do and don't do as Christians. But as Andy Stanley would say, "You better be careful about what you say about people who Jesus died for." Don't judge other people just because they sin differently from you! My prayer is God will draw you to Jesus, and you will fall eternally in love with Him. Remember salvation is in Jesus Christ alone with nothing else added!

FOR PERSONAL REFLECTION AND DISCUSSION

- Does your church have a "to do" list? What's on it?
- What did the thief on the cross do?
- What performance do you think is required for salvation? Why?

32

God Equips Us

I had an idea for a book about all the things people believe about God that just aren't true. I submitted that manuscript to a literary agent in hopes he would represent me with publishers. He read my manuscript and gave me feedback. He didn't like the premise or theme of the book, although he must have liked some of the manuscript, because he agreed to represent me if I was willing to change (rewrite) the book.

I prayed about it and realized he was right. I had been writing my book. It needed to be rewritten so it would be His book. It was as if God said to me, "Don't tell people why they're wrong, just tell them about Me." And the idea for this book was born. And the Lord has given His words. He is equipping me to write a book about Him.

There is a growing misconception that the best place to serve God is in an area where you have some training, a particular skill set, or a great interest or passion. And that makes sense from a human perspective. But I haven't found any examples in the Bible of God calling specially equipped or trained people. God calls people and then equips them for the job.

If you look at many of the characters in the Bible, they had no background skill set or training for what God called them to do. Here are a few examples:

• **Noah**—God did not choose Noah to build the Ark because he was a master shipbuilder. God chose Noah because he was a righteous man and walked faithfully with God. God equipped Noah to build the Ark and gave him specific instructions on how to do it.

• **Abraham**—At age 75, God told Abraham that He was going to make him into a great nation. God told Abraham, "Go to the land I will show you." And Abraham packed up and left. He didn't know where he was going; he was just obeying God. Later, God gave Abraham a son in his old age. His wife Sarah was in her 90s and past normal childbearing years. They named their son Isaac, and through him, a great nation was built. Abraham had no training for the job; he just believed God and God counted it to him as righteousness.

• **Moses**—Moses had killed an Egyptian man and fled to Midian to hide from Pharaoh, who was trying to kill him. Later, while Moses was still in Midian, God spoke to him at the burning bush and told Moses He had seen the plight of the Israelites, and He was going to rescue them from slavery. Great news for the Israelites! Then, God said to Moses, "So now, go. I am sending you to Pharaoh to bring my people the Israelites out of Egypt." Moses argued with God because he didn't think he was qualified for the job. He told God he was not an eloquent speaker. He tried his best to wiggle out of the assignment God had given him. Eventually, Moses did go to Pharaoh and demanded the release of the Israelites. God equipped Moses for the job He had called him to do. And if you look closely at the text, you will see God told Moses, "So I have come down to rescue them from the hand of the Egyptians." God said He was going to do it; He wasn't telling Moses to do it alone. God was going to do it and would use Moses as the messenger in the process. So, God didn't choose Moses because Moses was skilled at the job. God equipped Moses to do the job for which He had called him.

• **Paul** - Paul was a Pharisee, a Jew's Jew. His mission was to persecute the new Christians. Then, on the way to Damascus, he encountered Jesus (Acts 9). His eyes were opened to the truth that Jesus was, in fact, the long-expected Messiah. Paul immediately began to preach in the synagogues that Jesus was the Son of God. Paul was the least likely person to preach about Jesus, given that days earlier, he was persecuting the Christians. Paul had no expertise in preaching the Gospel, especially to the Jews. As it turned out, Peter preached the Gospel mostly to the Jews, while Paul preached the Gospel mostly to the Gentiles (non-Jews). But God equipped him for the job God had called him to do.

• **Peter**—Peter was a fisherman by trade. Jesus told Peter to "Follow me." Peter had no training to be a disciple. The night before Jesus' crucifixion, three times he denied he even knew Jesus. But Jesus commissioned him to be the head of His church! Jesus would equip Peter for the job God had called him to do.

• **Matthew**—Matthew was a tax collector and despised by most Jews because of his job. Nobody likes paying taxes, even today. What did Matthew know about being a disciple? He was an unlikely person to be chosen by Jesus as an apostle. Yet, he left his job and followed Jesus. Later, he would be equipped to do the job God had called him to do.

• **Luke**—Luke was a medical doctor. What did he know about being a disciple? Yet he followed Jesus, just like Peter and Matthew. And Jesus equipped all four of them to become apostles to preach the Good News after Jesus returned to His Father in heaven. All four of them went on to write many of the books in the Bible. What did they know about writing books? But God prepared them to write.

The point to be made is if God calls you to a particular service (ministry), He will equip you to perform the job successfully. Don't reject God's call simply because you don't feel qualified to do it.

Having said that, you should know there is nothing wrong with gift-based service. If you have a degree in accounting and your church needs an accountant in their finance department, then that is a place where you could serve. Or if you're a school teacher and there is a need for a Sunday school teacher, that is a logical place for you to serve.

But gift-based service is not the only way to serve God. I want you to know if God calls you to some service, He will equip you to do the job. It is impossible for God to fail. He always accomplishes His purpose. And sometimes He wants to accomplish that purpose through you!

If God calls you to do it—He will equip you for it. After all, I'm writing this book!!

FOR PERSONAL REFLECTION AND DISCUSSION

- What are your spiritual gifts? How are you using them?
- Has God ever called you to do something and then equipped you for it?
- In your opinion, does a "need" constitute a "call"? Why, why not?

33

God Can Be Trusted

In my early years as an entrepreneur, God blessed my business financially. But after about three years, revenue started to drop, and it kept dropping. All the things we had done in the past to generate sales just were no longer working. I went into debt to keep the business going. Finally, the creditors were banging on my door, the bank was about to foreclose on my house, and my car was about to be repossessed.

I prayed, "Okay, Lord, if this is what you require of me then so be it. If You need to take everything, including my pride, dignity, and self-worth, then You can have it all. My trust is still in You." I was like Jehoshaphat when he prayed, "Lord, our enemies are all around us, and I don't know what to do. But my eyes are on you."

I wish I could tell you the next day I found a check for $1 million in my mailbox but I can't. However, things slowly began to get better. After a year, the business was back to where it was originally, and even growing faster than we had expected. During that time period, I never stopped trusting God. I now tell people it was my most profitable year—I learned so much about trusting in God and depending on Him for virtually everything. It deepened my faith and my relationship with God.

I have to admit, though, when I was first married, I did not give regularly to my church. We were young and money was tight. We had small children, and they cost more than milk, diapers, and Kleenex. Today I'm not proud of that, but it's the truth.

At work, I pledged money from my paycheck to United Way

each payday. When I did a little research about them, I discovered a very high percentage of the money donated went to administrative functions and not to needy recipients. So, I researched other charitable organizations and learned many others also had high administrative costs. I kept searching and found an organization that gave the most of my donation to actual needy people, and I started donating to them instead.

Then, one Sunday morning my pastor gave a sermon on giving. He spoke of tithing 10% of your income to the church. What? I thought that was impossible because my budget was already very tight. He directed us to open our Bibles to Malachi 3:8-12. God told His people they were robbing Him. They asked, "How are we robbing you?" God replied, "In tithes and offerings. Bring the whole tithe (10%) into the storehouse, so there may be food in my house."

I remember wondering how in the world I could do that on my budget. Then, the pastor read further where God said, "Test me in this! And see if I will not throw open the floodgates of heaven and pour out so much blessing there will not be enough room to store it."

God was challenging me to test Him! He was challenging me to give 10% and see what happened. So, I decided in my heart to consider accepting God's challenge—but the pastor kept preaching. He walked down from the pulpit and handed a $20 bill to Mike, who was sitting in the front row, and he asked Mike to just hold it for him, which Mike did.

A few minutes later, he asked Mike to give the $20 bill to Mary, who was seated a few rows behind him. He asked Mary to hold the $20 for him and Mary did. A few minutes later, he asked Mary to give the $20 bill to Sam, seated a few rows away and across the aisle. After a few more minutes, the offering plate was passed around, and he asked Sam to put the $20 bill in the offering plate, which Sam did.

Before the end of the service, the pastor asked Mike, "Did you have any trouble giving the $20 to Mary?" Mike said no. Next, he asked Mary if she had any trouble giving the $20 to Sam, and Mary said no. Then, he asked Sam if he had any trouble putting the $20 in the offering plate. Sam said no. The pastor asked if any of us knew why none of them had any trouble giving away the $20 bill. The answer was, "They never felt like the $20 was their money!"

None of them had ever thought of the money as theirs. Then he explained everything we have comes from God—even our money. And when we think of our money as His money, we won't have any trouble giving it away—because it was really never ours in the first place.

I knew right then I would trust God and start giving 10% of my income to God. I would take God up on His challenge and see what happened. It was a giant leap of faith for me! At first, it was a little bit of a struggle, but gradually, tithing got easier. Then, things started to happen! I got a raise at work, eventually paid off my car, and soon our budget was comfortable with giving 10% to my church.

Today, it's the first check I write every month. I don't even think about. And over the years, the 10% will get bigger and bigger because 10% of thousands is more than 10% of hundreds. And I don't begrudge God one nickel. It's all His anyway. You came into the world with nothing, and you will go out with nothing. Everything in between comes from Him anyway.

As I matured in my faith, I became more targeted in my giving. Instead of just putting my tithe in the offering plate, I found out what the church needed, which missionaries they supported, as well as other needs, and how they were spending my tithes. Sometimes if they needed some new computers, I would buy them and donate them to the church. Sometimes I would send money directly to certain missionaries.

I targeted my money where I felt God wanted the money to go.

As my faith grew, I became a cheerful giver, and the blessings in my life continued to flourish because I had become a good steward of God's money.

Perhaps you've had a bad experience with your church or with a charitable organization. Perhaps you've stopped giving altogether. I urge you to take up God's challenge. Test Him and see what happens. I read somewhere we should give, then give until it hurts, then keep giving until it doesn't hurt anymore. God is forever faithful, and you can trust Him to keep His promises.

So, instead of thinking you can't trust the church with your money, perhaps it would be better to ask, "Can God trust me with His money?"

FOR PERSONAL REFLECTION AND DISCUSSION

- Have you ever tested God in regards to your giving?
- Is giving important to you? Why, why not?
- What does it mean to be a "cheerful" giver? Are you a cheerful giver?

34

From Manger to Cross

When I was a little girl, the anticipation of Christmas caused me to fold the pages down on the Sears Christmas catalog and hope something on my Christmas list magically appeared on Christmas morning. Our family tradition was to write our letters to Santa after the Macy's Thanksgiving parade. As I grew older, I helped my younger sisters and brother to write their individual letters.

When I was a teenager, we were singing Christmas carols one afternoon and my next to the youngest sister was sad. When Mom asked her what was wrong, my sister Joan said, "It's not fair! We always sing Christmas Carols, but we never sing Christmas Joanie's!" (You need to know that my next oldest sister was named Carol!)

The big deal at Easter was our special hats and coats and all the Easter eggs, marshmallow chicks, and chocolate bunnies. When I became an adult, these holidays didn't have much special meaning. Of course, the entire family went to Mass on Christmas morning and Easter Sunday because that is what you were supposed to do. I was oblivious to any other possible meaning of these two holidays.

To many people, Christmas is an enigma. There are those enthusiasts that start decorating their yards and homes before Halloween arrives. Some overly zealous Christmas shoppers start their shopping in January for the coming year (when all the after-Christmas sales appear and prices are lower). Others are knee-deep in preparing Christmas concerts, Christmas plays, Christmas pageants, Christmas caroling, Christmas parties, etc. It is the season of secular busyness.

Sadly, others look forward to Christmas with dread. For those who have lost loved ones, there may be little joy in Christmas for them. For families parted by war, there is a missing parent on Christmas morning, who will not see their children opening presents. Others are in physical and emotional pain in hospitals with serious illnesses, who cannot come home for Christmas. Still others are in nursing homes, where no one comes to visit them for Christmas. Loneliness and confusion are daily companions to those with dementia who can't remember what Christmas is all about.

But, regardless of your perspective, most people know the story about angels singing and a stable and a baby Jesus and shepherds. They know the story by heart, and many go to church to celebrate the birth of Jesus. But, alas, like I used to do, many people leave it there and don't understand what the big deal is about Christmas.

The wonder and miracle of Christmas centers on Jesus Christ, the only Son of God. He laid aside His deity to become a human being, born of a woman, and physically entered the earth as a tiny baby. God became a man, and the Creator became subject to His creation. Jesus came as fully divine and fully human to walk in our footsteps and feel our pain and joy and fear and doubt in His humanity. He was a man of sorrows for all of us!

When Jesus was 30 years old, He began His public ministry. Jesus proclaimed the Good News of the Gospel to everyone everywhere He went. He took time alone daily to pray to His Father in heaven and was refreshed and prepared to face the next day. He spoke what He heard the Father said, did what He saw the Father doing, and trusted His Father completely with His life. He preached the Gospel of love and forgiveness and healed people, both physically and spiritually.

Christmas is a warm fuzzy for people who love it because it is the story of a newborn baby and happiness, etc. At this point, it is easy to accept and celebrate His birth because it doesn't cost us anything. We can observe the events, but we don't have to react to them by making a special commitment to God.

However, Easter is another story! The comfortable place is seen in the rites of spring—Easter bunnies and eggs and baby ducks and all kinds of beautiful flowers in the spring when God's creations are waking up from their winter naps. Easter's true meaning is when we celebrate the crucifixion and resurrection of Jesus, which offends some people and threatens the status quo.

The event marks the end of Jesus' earthly life and His return to heaven to sit down at the right hand of God the Father. His resurrection completed God's plan to offer salvation to all mankind because the death of Jesus paid the price God required for all sin!

The difficulty in celebrating Easter in its redemptive sense is you have to admit you are a sinner. You have to admit you have been running your life on your own terms up to this time. Like Frank Sinatra, you've done it your way! Easter offers you the opportunity to accept these facts about yourself and realize you are lost in your sins and cannot stop sinning by your own self-effort.

Even your small, seemingly insignificant sins make you a sinner. Maybe you think gossiping, telling little white lies, or taking pens and paper from your workplace is not a big deal—everyone does it. But as Jesus stretched out His arms on the cross, He was dying for those little, insignificant sins as well as for those big sins like murder, rape, lying, etc.

In the Catholic ritual of the Stations of the Cross on Good Friday, the day Jesus died, you walk through the 14 stations, each depicting the final steps of Jesus before and after His horrific death. He was scourged with leaded whips, and a woven crown of thorns was smashed onto His head.

He had to carry His cross most of the way to the place of His crucifixion. The soldiers nailed Him to the cross with long heavy nails, and the cross was raised for all to see. His disciples ran away, and He was utterly alone in His agony– even His Father had to look away. Jesus had become "sin" and was the sacrificial Lamb of God to satisfy God's justice and accomplish the plan of salvation. It was the supreme act of God's love for us!

So, to celebrate Easter properly, you have to do some serious soul searching. You cannot view it from the stands. No one else can do it for you—only you can decide about choosing the free gift of life in God and become a forgiven sinner. Once you have decided to accept Jesus as your Lord and Savior, you will experience true freedom, the peace that surpasses all understanding, and a joy no one can take from you! How profound is that?

So, these two major holidays mark the beginning and the end of Jesus' life on earth. They commemorate the eternal legacy He left behind for all mankind. That's the big deal! I remember a pastor once told his congregation when closing his sermon on Easter Sunday, "For those of you who I won't see again until next Easter—Merry Christmas and Happy New Year."

These two events are so significant, we mark our calendars by them. Join in the celebration and be part of God's love and forgiveness. This gift is good all year round, and there are no annual renewals! That's the best gift in the world, and it keeps on giving every day of your life!

FOR PERSONAL REFLECTION AND DISCUSSION

- How has the commercialization of Christmas affected the way you celebrate?
- Picture yourself at the manger. How would you have felt?
- Picture yourself at the foot of the cross. How would you have felt?

35

Agreeing With God

I'm sure you've heard the old adage, "Confession is good for the soul." Well, I believe it's true! We've all seen movies where one character is keeping a secret from another person. And in the end, they always confess their secrets. It's like getting it off your chest or "I just can't stand this anymore so I had to tell you."

Perhaps you saw the movie Mrs. Doubtfire starring Robin Williams. When he and his wife (Sally Field) divorced, she got custody of the children. He was so devastated he applied for the job of her nanny disguised as a woman (Mrs. Doubtfire) so he could be near his children. In the end, of course, his lie is uncovered. He feels relief because he no longer needs to maintain the lie. And the audience feels a big sense of relief that the masquerade is over.

That is what confession is like. It's like confessing your sins to God just gets it off your chest. It gives you a basis for moving forward. Confession is just agreeing with God about your sin. God already knows I did it, so my confession is just agreeing with Him about that fact.

One of the functions of the Holy Spirit is to convict us of sin. I remember, as a non-believer, when I was first convicted of my sin. It was an oppressive feeling. I knew for the first time in my life I was a sinner—a big time sinner, and I was overwhelmed with guilt. I just knew I needed forgiveness for my sin. I had heard before Jesus had died for my sins, but I had never really accepted His death as the free gift of forgiveness from God. I was really desperate!

I rushed to get a Bible. Instinctively I just opened it to the middle, and it fell open to the 25th Psalm. I started reading and was stunned when I got to verse 4 which said, "Show me your ways, Lord. Teach me your paths. Guide me in your truth and teach me, for you are my God, my Savior." That was it—I knew in that instant Christ's death on the cross was for my sins! I fell to my knees on my living room floor at 3:00 a.m. in the morning, in tears, and accepted Christ as my Lord and Savior.

At that moment, I asked God to forgive me for my sins. And somehow, I just knew my sins—past, present, and future—were all forgiven. My tears changed immediately from remorse/repentance to absolute joy over knowing my sins were forgiven!

It was just a huge relief to go from being a sinner to being forgiven. That was the most glorious day of my life. For the first time in my life, I knew I had been blind, but now I could see. Everything had changed!

After that day, I would become convicted of my new sins. And every time the Holy Spirit would point out some sin to me, I would immediately ask for forgiveness. As I matured in my faith, I became aware of many new truths the Holy Spirit continued to show me. I was a sponge, soaking up all I could about God. One of the things I learned was I didn't need to ask forgiveness every time I sinned.

The Bible said, "If we confess our sins, He is faithful and just and will forgive us our sins, and purify us from all unrighteousness" (1 John 1:9). My sins were already forgiven—at the Cross. I just needed to confess them to God. My confession was simply agreeing with God about my sin. And I believe my confession is probably more for my benefit than God's. It gives me a new starting place and a peace, knowing God and I are on the same page.

But notice the two things about God after that in the verse— "He is faithful and just to forgive our sins." Faithfulness means He will never stop forgiving us for our sins. He is absolutely faithful about it. That is just who He is! But He is also justified in forgiving us our sins. He is justified in forgiving us because Christ has already paid the penalty for our sins. Our sins don't need to be paid for twice, so God is just when He forgives our sin.

As a Christian, you are already forgiven. You don't need to ask for forgiveness every time you sin. So just confess (agree with God), repent, and move on with your life!

FOR PERSONAL REFLECTION AND DISCUSSION

- When does God forgive your sin?
- Why is confession important to God? Why is it important to you?
- How does being forgiven make you feel?

36

Labor With Him

In 1956 my father built the house in which I grew up. Later, as an adult, my younger brother wanted to build a new house for himself and his family. My father naturally got recruited due to his expertise, and my youngest son and I also got recruited. My dad was retired, and my youngest son was fifteen and out of school for the summer. They were both able to work full-time six days each week.

My brother and I were only available on Friday afternoons and Saturdays because we both had jobs during the week. We weren't building the house for him; we were building the house with him. It's the same way with God. God doesn't want us to work *for* Him; He wants us to work *with* Him.

Within our human nature, God has given us the capacity to have compassion for others. As babies we go through the terrible twos of being selfish and demanding. For most of us, we grow out of that stage and become more aware of the needs of other people around us. We begin to share our toys and give other children the right to go first down the slide.

Joyce remembers when her sister, Carol, who was about four years old at the time, was upset because she didn't have a gift for her mother for Mother's Day. She took her bedspread off her bed and gave it to Mom as a gift of love!

It is said no child is born prejudiced but learns that unwholesome trait through the views and behaviors of parents, siblings, classmates, TV shows, etc. But the innate characteristic of compassion in our humanity shows through these prejudices and kicks into gear when we sense someone is in danger. We don't even think about it—for example, we snatch the elderly person to safety who is starting to walk in front of a car; we dive into the swimming pool and rescue the endangered child; we step in to stop a fight between a small-sized child and a bully. It's all very natural, instinctive behavior. We are there to help!

When we accept Jesus Christ as our Lord and Savior, we are overwhelmed by His forgiveness, mercy, grace, love, and blessing! We want everyone we know to experience the same thing we did. We want to save the world!

John 4 recounts Jesus meeting the Samaritan woman at Jacob's well. In verses 25-30, she tells Jesus that the Messiah is coming, and He would declare all things to them. Jesus replied that He was the Messiah! She leaves her water pot at the well and ran into the city and said, "Come, see a man who told me all the things that I had done; this is not the Christ, is it?" Her response to Jesus' love was to run and tell others!

Many people feel overly compelled to share their conversion experience with others. They want to drag them into salvation themselves, whether or not they want to be saved. They often think it is their job alone to bring someone to Christ—that it is a solo project. After all, many of us came to salvation because someone shared their testimony, or we heard someone like Billy Graham give an altar call after a sermon.

Andrew heard Jesus speak and went and brought his brother, Simon Peter, to Jesus. Only Jesus could invite Simon Peter to follow Him (John 1:35-42). But, in reality, salvation is always a partnership between you and God. You can't save anyone, but God certainly can! You can share your testimony and pray for their salvation and hope God answers that prayer and offers His gift of salvation. Only they can accept their salvation from God. God does not have any grandchildren, only children.

Jesus tells a Parable of the Sower in Matthew 13:3-23. The

sower scatters his seed all over—some fell by the road and the birds ate them up; some fell on rocky places that had little soil, and they germinated but withered because they had no root; some fell among thorns, and the thorns choked them out; and some fell on good soil and yielded a bumper crop. The seed was scattered, but the results were starkly different from one another!

Because God has given us the gift of free will, we can never coerce someone into meeting God and accepting His gift of salvation. We cannot argue with someone to get them saved. Only God can know someone's heart and if they are ready to be the good soil to receive the seed of His salvation or not. Your testimony of coming to faith can plant the seed of God's salvation—that is your role in the process.

God doesn't expect you to be *successful* in sharing your faith. God desires you to be *faithful* and share your faith with others. God will do the saving, taking all the pressure off you for having to create results. You can relax, share your faith in a loving way, and leave the rest to Him. Don't feel like you're working for God. Relax, share your faith in a loving way, and then let God do His part. Laboring with Him is the idea. God wants to be involved in all you do.

Also, understand you cannot be the giver of the gift that is not yours to give. Jesus alone earned that right to give that gift on the cross. The recipient must choose to accept it through his/her free will. Romans 6:23 says, "For the wages of sin is death, but the free gift of God is eternal life in Christ Jesus our Lord." Philemon 1:1 explains, "but without your consent, I did not want to do anything, so that your goodness would not be, in effect, by compulsion but of your own free will."

In 1 Corinthians 13:8-9 (the famous chapter on love), Paul says that gifts of prophecy, tongues, and knowledge will pass away, but love—God's love and His gift of love—never fails. Whoever asks for God's gift of salvation will receive it! We can't give others our salvation, but we can make them want it.

I believe the call on anyone's life is to be an example of what a Christian life should be as a living testimony of God at work. Being a Christian is not a piece of cake or a sure way to avoid suffering in this life. Jesus tells us to pick up our cross and follow Him. Challenges are guaranteed to come your way. Your witness of Jesus in your life is how you handle these challenges with Jesus on your side.

Part of Joyce's personal cross included going through a divorce, being a single mom, losing a job, and losing her only child as an adult to drugs. God walked her through each one of those situations and comforted her in her sorrow. God gave her the grace to come out of each tragedy as a more sensitive, caring woman who could empathize with others that had experienced the same losses.

People who knew her could see how Jesus interacted with her confusion and grief and exchanged all that stuff for His mercy and peace. They saw the fruit of God's salvation in her life from the seed He planted.

None of the healing happened overnight—it was a daily, one baby step at a time kind of journey. How reassuring to someone who is in the midst of confusion or even apathy to see what Jesus can do in someone else's life! So, you don't have to be a successful witness. You just have to be a faithful witness and share your faith in love and leave to rest to God."

As we live in the light of His love, we are to show His love to others—we are His hands and His feet on earth. But we cannot begin that walk until we have accepted God's gift of salvation. Take some time to spend with God in prayer and reading your Bible and see who He wants you to be. Once saved, you can share the joy of His perfect gift with anyone! You do the sharing, and He'll do the saving!

FOR PERSONAL REFLECTION AND DISCUSSION

- Have you ever shared the Gospel with someone? Describe the experience.
- In your opinion, what is the difference between faithful and successful?
- If you were arrested for being a Christian, would there be enough evidence to convict you? Explain.

37

God Cares About Me

Many years ago, I went through a time of Christian therapy regarding my sexual abuse. I remember feeling like I was suspended in an abyss—no top, no bottom, no light at either end of the tunnel. I was held captive in my mind with my trauma like a deer paralyzed by the headlights. Through God's grace and mercy, I am healed from that entire trauma!

Have you ever felt lonely or isolated or abandoned? There are certainly many situations out of your control that promote and create those feelings in your mind and heart.

Many of us feel alone in a crowd of people, hiding in our protective shell and oblivious to everyone and everything around us. Sometimes that survival technique can become your daily behavior and existence. If this happens to you all the time, you might be dwelling in the midst of mental depression where the sun does not shine, there are no blue clouds in the sky, and life is meaningless.

The ultimate expression of deep depression is thoughts of suicide: physical suicide where you kill yourself or clinical suicide where you run away from everything and everyone in your life. You can even imagine God wouldn't care if you died. You feel it wouldn't make any difference to Him or the world if suddenly you weren't alive.

A story has circulated on Facebook about a little boy named Teddy Stoddard and his fifth grade teacher, Mrs. Thompson. To Mrs. Thompson, Teddy was a problem student because of his appearance, lack of hygiene habits, and inability to participate effectively in class in learning the lessons. At first she felt some plea-sure in giving Teddy a grade of "F" on his test papers.

Then she learned Teddy's mother had died when he was in third grade, and he was totally lost without her and did not have a happy home life. Mrs. Thompson felt guilty about how she had treated Teddy, began to spend more time helping him with his studies, and discovered Teddy was very bright.

That Christmas, Teddy gave her a special bracelet missing some stones and an almost empty bottle of perfume. When she put the bracelet on her wrist and dabbed the perfume behind her ears, Teddy told her she smelled just like his mother, and she was the best teacher ever.

From then on, she stopped teaching only spelling and arith-metic, and started teaching children. She kept track of Teddy's progress in school as he finished elementary school and placed third in his senior year class in high school. He went on to college and excelled in his grades, taking several extra years of study to become a licensed physician. He wrote her letters memorializing every milestone in his life and always repeated that she was the best teacher he ever had.

When Teddy got married shortly after medical school gradua-tion, he asked Mrs. Thompson to come to his wedding and sit in the place reserved for the groom's mother. She came and wore the bracelet and the perfume he gave her in the fifth grade. What an in-credible story of someone who was lost and marginalized and the results of having someone who really cared for him and encour-aged him to be all he could be. Mrs. Thompson believed in Teddy and nurtured him and encouraged him—what an extraordinary dif-ference that made in his life!

When Mrs. Thompson first met Teddy, she was convinced he was disposable as a student, and she focused on the other students. To her credit, she checked Teddy's first four years of school and became aware of his history. She saw that he had the ability to be a good student but was totally lost by the death of his mother in the third grade.

Mrs. Thompson realized you should never judge a book by its cover! The extra time she spent with him was exactly what Teddy needed and spurred him on to excel in elementary school, high school, and beyond. To him, Mrs. Thompson would always be the best teacher because she took a special interest in him!

After his mom died, Teddy felt no one cared about him and his success or failure. After accepting Mrs. Thompson's encouragement and friendship, Teddy finally realized the sky was the limit, and he decided to go for it! The best part of the story for me was when Teddy invited Mrs. Thompson to come to his wedding and sit in the mother-of-the-groom seat. She came and wore his mother's rhinestone bracelet and her perfume, which she had kept all those years.

The truth is God has loved you from the foundation of the earth and has a wonderful purpose for your life. He made you in His image and formed every part of you in your mother's womb (Psalm 139:13-17 NASB). He is omnipresent (is everywhere) and omniscient (knows everything) and has laid His hand upon you (Psalm 139:1-12 NASB). God says that He has a plan for your life and your welfare, not to bring calamity to you but to give you a future and a hope (Jer. 29:11-14 NASB).

Wow, He has a blueprint plan for your life that is yours free of charge! You can understand the purpose for your life if you ask Jesus Christ to be your Savior and Lord. He will guide you as you walk with Him and get to know Him personally. He will help you to open your heart to receive His purpose for you.

If you have ever put together jigsaw puzzles, especially the 1000-piece ones, you probably have encountered a situation when you have faithfully labored for days in putting it together, only to discover you are missing one piece! All that work and the puzzle could not be completed until you find that piece.

In God's plan for mankind, all of us are puzzle pieces essential to completing His plan. Because you have the choice to decide whether or not to go with God's plan, you can wrongly decide God and the world don't need you—if you died tomorrow, no one would miss you. But, the puzzle could never be finished without you!

When you are really down on yourself and depressed to the extent you feel you could never make any difference in your immediate world or the world at large, it's almost impossible to lift up your eyes to anything different than what you are experiencing. The good news is that as a born-again Christian, you can lift up your eyes to the hills from where your help comes from God Himself (Psalm 121:1-8 NASB).

He doesn't have an answering service or voice mail for your cry for help. He is there for you at any time at any place from which you call on Him. You don't need to memorize standard formal prayers. My most simple prayer to God sometimes is "Help"! He always answers me, and I know He watches over me and loves me unconditionally as my heavenly Father!

God made you for a distinct purpose that only you can fulfill. This purpose is unique to you, and it encompasses everything you have ever experienced. You can make a difference and give answers and hope to others who have shared in your fears, disappointments, shattered hopes and dreams, and tragic losses. Your brokenness can actually be an answer for someone.

Your story is called your witness or testimony of how God made a difference in your life. He loves you and cares for you beyond anything you can imagine!

FOR PERSONAL REFLECTION AND DISCUSSION

- What made Mrs. Thompson a better teacher?
- Have you ever felt lonely or abandoned? Describe.
- How can the story of Mrs. Thompson make you a better person?

38

God in Our Schools

Since the United States constitution was written almost 250 years ago, we have seen the gradual erosion of Christianity in our country. Today, God seems unwelcome in most places outside of church. Nowhere has this erosion been more prevalent and more impacting than in our public schools.

Many years ago, schools at all age levels promoted the American ideals of our Constitution. Boys were boys, and girls were girls. There was order and not chaos. Teaching the three Rs—reading, writing and 'rithmetic—were the foundational cornerstones of elementary school. Upper grades learned about history, civics, social studies, science, and the fine arts. Universities taught actual knowledge, not opinions or movements.

Unfortunately, today there are many among us who are illiterate (can't read or write properly). This group is painfully unaware of American and world history. Many young people today cannot think for themselves, form their own opinions, or establish a personal life philosophy. I believe this happened because God was taken out of our school systems.

The Pledge of Allegiance and the Constitution are the bedrock and foundation of our unique culture. The Founding Fathers included God in these two documents and others because this nation was founded under God. We were a Christian nation, and the world recognized us as such a nation. There was little or no disagreement about who we were and the God we worshipped.

In current times, however, everything we knew and loved has

drastically changed! There are hot spots all over the country that demand you to give up your rights to "life, liberty and the pursuit of happiness" and substitute a new culture of socialism, which has no place for God at all. In a gradual takeover, God has been rudely and deliberately ushered out of the school systems.

Prayer is now not allowed in public schools at any level—even graduating valedictorians cannot use a prayer in their graduation speeches. Children are no longer allowed to acknowledge God in reciting the Pledge of Allegiance because that pledge has been dropped by most public schools.

Students also see football stars and other sports figures kneeling during the singing of our national anthem! What message are we giving our children?

Under the threat of socialism, anxiety and confusion have been rampant in school bathrooms and locker rooms. Parents and teachers alike have raised concerns regarding bullying and safety at school.

For some time, the federal government has intervened in what courses schools are allowed to teach their students, and on the whole, have not been successful. These methods have caused students to depend almost totally on a calculator, a computer, or an iPhone without a teacher's input.

The atmosphere in public schools has morphed from learning basic knowledge skills to absorbing re-written history and the opinions of teachers and professors. It is difficult to find truth or history in the classrooms!

God is a respecter of people, and He will never intervene where He is not wanted. He will withdraw His hand of blessings from any group of people who don't want anything to do with Him or His Word. As a result, school boards today have an attitude of "I know what's best for your kids." Our schools are reeling and trying to decide what the meaning of actual truth is today. God watches from heaven and longs to give us His plan for our children's education.

The job of parents and teachers alike is to nurture the children in their charge. God Himself is a Father of all mankind, and His delight is in His children. His law provides standards of morality for both young children and adults. His peaceful presence offers an atmosphere of order, peace, respect, compassion, and freedom, allowing children to be all they can be. He encourages children to learn and to do their best through godly teachers.

God provides compassion for difficult circumstances in a child's home-life and helps students feel safe in the classroom under the teacher's charge. As you read in the last chapter, Mrs. Thompson taught Teddy more than book learning—she taught him to believe in himself and to shoot for the stars. God does the same thing for all of His children, regardless of their age.

God not only teaches respect for others but self-respect for every child. Instead of shouting down other students, drowning out every voice but their own, God instructs them to listen to one another and take turns in talking. God encourages His children, big or small, to work together in unity, not fighting for superiority or status. He encourages the older students to watch out for the younger ones. He gives spiritual protection to the teachers, so they feel safe and peaceful in their classrooms.

The education children need today is less about math, science, and history and more about good character. While we can't teach about God in the classroom today, we can certainly teach His virtues of honesty, integrity, love your neighbor, generosity, kindness, forgiveness, and equality. What do you think might happen in our country if our kids had these concepts as the foundations of their life philosophies?

The absence of God in schools has led to an explosion in homeschooling. Steve's youngest daughter homeschools her twin boys and has since they became school age. She and her husband just did not like what was being taught in the schools—and largely what was not being taught. They faithfully have Bible studies as part of their daily curriculum. This trend is likely to continue.

There will never be "heaven on earth" in schools or homes or workplaces, but they can be positive sanctuaries of Christian virtues to be learned and passed on to others. God is compassionate and gracious; He is slow to anger and abounding in loving-kindness (Psalm 103:8).

Paul writes in 1 Corinthians 13:3-7 (NASB),

Love is patient, love is kind and is not jealous; love does not brag and is not arrogant, does not act unbecomingly; it does not seek its own, is not provoked, does not take into account a wrong suffered, does not rejoice in unrighteousness, but rejoices with the truth; bears all things; believes all things; hopes all things; endures all things.

God's presence in the classroom can comfort and encourage students who have a miserable home life. His presence can inspire and encourage a student to reach for the stars. His presence in the classroom needs to be reinstated for the sake of future generations!

FOR PERSONAL REFLECTION AND DISCUSSION

- Why do you think God has been kicked out of our schools?
- What do you think it will take to get God back in our schools?
- Why do you think God's relevance in the U.S. has decreased in the last 50 years?

39

Abdicating My Throne

As an early baby boomer, I grew up in a family with seven children and a stay-at-home mom. Being the oldest child had its own set of rules of how my life was ordered under the strict control of my parents. I was to set the example to my younger siblings, and I had to walk a fine line with little tolerance for doing my own thing.

Because of finances, I commuted to and from college and finally left home in the second semester of my senior year to be free to live my own life. My self-esteem and how I felt about myself were in tatters at this point. Self-preservation became my attempt to establish my kingdom of self where I made my own rules and lived my own life.

Something deep within the human personality wants to be free of any law or restraint that limits its own mindset, offers common sense, and tries to change our mind about anything or everything. I based many of my life views on my feelings and emotions—these parts of my personality shaped and dictated my outlook on every aspect of life itself, and it suited me just fine, thank you very much! Does that sound familiar to you?

Something within our personalities involves a mighty kingdom of self that we establish in our terrible twos, and we become our own dictator-for-life for our personal kingdom. I want to live life on my terms—I know best what's good for me, and I don't need anyone's help or approval. I am perfectly content to work harder and not smarter.

As the Frank Sinatra song goes, "I'll do it my way!" In my kingdom, I hold all my truths to be self-evident—the right to life, liberty, and the pursuit of happiness on my terms. It's as if the famous American Revolution "Gadsden flag," depicting a coiled rattlesnake on a yellow background, displays the motto, "Don't tread on me!" and flies high over the castle of my self-kingdom.

The following is a famous quote in a sermon by 17th century English author John Donne: "No man is an island unto himself! No one is self-sufficient; everyone relies on others." God the Father created mankind to intermingle with people in all areas of our lives. This intermingling is like a strong wind that sweeps across our kingdom and wreaks havoc on our self-kingdom mindset with war, disease, loss of loved ones, jobs, or homes, misunderstandings, etc. All these things are beyond our control, and once they happen, we have to deal with the problems and the resulting consequences. Yikes!

God, our heavenly Father, offers some wisdom and solutions in the Bible. Luke 12:16-21 (NASB) tells us a parable of Jesus:

> *The land of a rich man was very productive. And he began reasoning to himself, saying "What shall I do, since I have no place to store my crops?" Then he said, "This is what I will do: I will tear down my barns and build larger ones, and there I will store all my grain and my goods. And I will say to my soul, 'Soul, you have many goods laid up for many years to come, take your ease, eat, drink and be merry!'"*

> *But God said to him, "You fool! This very night your soul is required of you, and now who will own what you have prepared?" So is the man who stores up treasure for himself and is not rich toward God.*

Whoa! That's a sobering thought! Then there is a portion of the Sermon on the Mount found in Matthew 7:24-27 (NASB):

Therefore, everyone who hears these words of Mine and acts on them, may be compared to a wise man who built his house on the rock. And the rain fell, and the floods came, and the winds blew and slammed against that house; and yet it did not fall, for it had been founded on the rock.

Everyone who hears these words of Mine and does not act on them, will be like a foolish man who built his house on the sand. The rain fell, and the floods came, and the winds blew and slammed against that house and it fell— and great was its fall.

These words of Jesus tell us what happens when we build our houses or kingdoms without God involved in it. Without using God's owner manual for our lives, we are destined to make horrendous mistakes, some of which can never be rectified or made better.

How does all this make you feel? I would be afraid, confused, fearful, and ready to abdicate my throne of self! So, building my own self-kingdom based on my feelings and emotions is destined for future disaster.

The reality is I do not know what's best for me based on my feelings. My feelings are not always based on the Bible, God's perfect truth! King Solomon, the wisest man who ever lived, wrote the Book of Proverbs about what wisdom is and how to obtain it. Chapter 1:2-6 (NASB) sets the goals of knowing wisdom and instruction, discerning sayings of understanding, and receiving instructions in wise behavior.

Proverbs gives guidance in righteousness, justice, and equity, giving prudence to the naïve and knowledge and discretion to youths of all ages. Chapter 1 further says, "The fear of the Lord (deep respect and reverence) is the beginning of knowledge; fools despise wisdom and instruction" (Proverbs 1:7 NASB).

Human nature tends to tell us our feelings are the truth. We feel tired or anxious about something, and that's the truth from our perspective. But other emotions, like guilt, may seem like the truth when maybe they aren't. In these cases, we face the dilemma of "Do I believe what I feel?" or "Do I believe what God says?"

God says, "You're forgiven," but you don't feel forgiven. So what do you believe—your feelings or what God says? In these cases, always go with what God says. Your feelings can't be trusted and aren't always the truth, but the Bible and what God says are always the truth. Just remember what you feel may not be the truth.

God's Word is not based on what you feel. In each of the four Gospels, Jesus' agony in the Garden of Gethsemane, before He was arrested by the Pharisees, was totally based on Jesus' human feelings. In His mental anguish, He asked His Father to spare Him from the crucifixion three distinct times. Yet, He also prayed all three times that His Father's will be done. He became obedient to God's will, even death on a cross, to become the Savior of all mankind!

Please understand that you are forgiven of your sins, and you are worthy to go to heaven NOT because of your feelings but because of what Jesus did on the cross at Calvary. That is the Gospel, and it is an undeniable fact. Truth is not what you feel; truth is what God says. After all, being the dictator of your self kingdom is insignificant compared to being a child of God on His throne. It's time to surrender to His truth and His love!

FOR PERSONAL REFLECTION AND DISCUSSION

- Why is self so hard to overcome? How do you overcome self?
- Why does the world glorify self?
- Give an example where you asked God for help because you couldn't do it alone.

40

"Just the Facts, Ma'am"

Perhaps you remember this famous line from Sergeant Joe Friday when he interrogated witnesses on the show *Dragnet*. Invariably his witnesses would want to embellish their stories to include many extraneous points, but Sergeant Friday would always remind them, "Just the facts, Ma'am, just the facts." And I remember my mother telling me as a kid, "If you can't say anything nice, then just don't say anything at all."

Maybe you heard your parents tell you the same thing. It's actually pretty good advice. The same advice applies when talking about the Bible—if it's not the facts, then don't say anything at all.

The Bible is full of stories, people, parables, laws, instructions, and much more. But the Bible is also silent about many things and, in some cases, open to different interpretations. This silence and interpretation are often the cause of debate between theologians and everyday Christians and probably why there are different Christian denominations today. Some of the past issues that have caused major divisions in the church include:

- The role of women in the church
- Homosexuality/brokenness
- The day to celebrate the Sabbath
- The way to properly baptize
- The frequency to celebrate communion
- Church administrative structure
- Allocation of church funds

And on and on it goes while the main focus of the Bible is the death and resurrection of Jesus Christ. In the Book of Acts and the rest of the New Testament, Paul and others set up the general concept of "church" for the infant Church at the time. We mustn't let more trivial issues overshadow our walk with God.

In some of the bullet points above, church policies regarding these items are decided within the denomination or church leadership. And remember these are just men and women like us, and we are entitled to our own interpretation of the Bible. All the points above should be based on scripture.

If God had wanted to answer every possible question that arose in the human mind, then the Bible would be bigger than all the books in the world combined. The Bible is the *Cliff Notes*. It is what God thought was essential for us to know. To me, it's as if God said, "Here is the important stuff. Get this right, and I'll share all the rest with you later, when you can better understand." So, I look at the Bible and try to get the important message God is conveying. And I think that message is summed up in four words— "Christ died for me!"

Once you realize how much God loves you, the rest of the Bible should be viewed with the backdrop of the cross. God loves everyone equally, and He sent Jesus to die for us while we all were still sinners. We need to love people and recognize many of them live in different situations than we do.

What matters is God loves all people, and He wants me to love them and to share the Gospel of salvation (Jesus) with them. Whether the Bible says a lifestyle or attitude is right or wrong is not my focus. What's important is that I love them and that I trust God to deal with their lifestyle.

Similarly, I don't care how you baptize—you can sprinkle, pour or dunk—the result is the same. Baptism is a public demonstration that you have died with Christ and share in His resurrection as a profession of faith. It isn't important what day of the week you call Sabbath but that you observe the day of rest and fellowship with other Christians in your church regularly. Whether you celebrate communion every week, every month, or twice a year is not as important as sharing in the communion Jesus created at the Last Supper in memory of Him.

My guiding principle is that if the Bible is silent about something, I should be silent about it too. If the Bible contains some things that are open to interpretation, then those issues can be debated. But debate should not lead to division. I don't believe God wants His people divided over something less significant than Christ's death and resurrection. I should not judge people because they sin differently than I do or have different ideas about how to "do church" than I have.

Jesus said, "Love your neighbor as yourself." He never said to debate every little thing, interpret every little thing, or cause division over little things. There are pillars of truth in our faith—the Virgin birth, Christ's death for my sins, His resurrection from the dead, and the Bible as the written Word of God.

If we can agree on these pillars of our faith, then we should not let anything else divide us. You can be free to believe whatever else you want, and I will still love you like a brother or sister. Then we can all let God help us to grow to be more like Jesus, regardless. I want you to know God loves you, and He does not want division. He wants us to love Him and love our neighbor as ourselves.

Paul said, "Three things remain—faith, hope, and love. But the greatest of these is love" (1 Corinthians 13:13). So, let love reign in your heart.

FOR PERSONAL REFLECTION AND DISCUSSION

- How do you explain things the Bible is unclear about?
- Does the Bible answer all questions? Why or why not?
- Is it okay for Christians to disagree? Why or why not?

41

Living the Christian Life

In 1961, a man from China named Watchman Nee wrote a book entitled *The Normal Christian Life.* In it he says the type of life most Christians live is not a normal Christian life. He suggests most Christians rarely attain the normal Christian life. It is an interesting perspective, but what does it mean?

I have been a Christian for over 50 years, and I've had struggles from time to time. Because of these struggles, I was curious to know Mr. Nee's definition of "normal." In my life, the Christian experience has been a never-ending repetition of peaks and valleys. Sometimes I've felt very close to God and, other times, not so much. It's certainly not been a continuous mountaintop experience. Was my experience what Mr. Nee would call "normal" or not?

Before I became a born-again Christian, I attended a church that, as Andy Stanley would say, "Was against everything." They were well-intended people who prayed regularly for my salvation. They told me Jesus had died for me, and there was nothing I needed to do because Jesus had already done everything. All I needed to do was believe.

Trusting in Christ and His work on the cross was my only requirement for spending eternity with Him in heaven. It sounded too easy, too good to be true! Certainly, there must be something I needed to do. Again, I was told nothing else needed to be done. Then one day, by God's grace, the truth was revealed to me, and I accepted Christ as my Lord and Savior. I was born-again and saved.

But after my conversion, they handed me a to-do list of all the things I needed to do. I needed to be baptized, start tithing, get in a Bible study, join the choir, etc. I was also given a list of things good Christians do not do—no more drinking, no more swearing, no more dancing (they were afraid it would lead to premarital sex), etc. So apparently, while there was nothing to do to get saved, there was a ton of things to do and not do after you were saved. Hmmm, that seemed very strange to me. They had said Jesus had done it all already. Apparently not.

Not knowing any better, I took both lists and started changing my life. Wasn't this the normal life Mr. Nee's book was about? Not so.

To me, the normal Christian life meant changing all the bad things about me and making them become good things via my self-effort. It didn't take long to realize I wasn't having much luck. I was failing at this Christian life. I kept asking forgiveness for the same sins over and over. I thought His yoke was supposed to be easy, and His burden was supposed to be light. It certainly didn't seem that way in my experience.

I knew my sins were forgiven, but I had no control over this sin generator that lived within me. I had no power over it. I was struggling to do all the things on the list that all good Christians do. Then one day I said, "God, I can't do this. I give up!" And I thought I heard God reply, "Finally you get it. You're not supposed to do it. You can't do it." This enlightenment from God encouraged me to start a great search to find out why I couldn't do it myself.

As I studied my Bible and read many books by scholarly Christian authors, the light began to brighten. In Isaiah 64:6, God says that all my righteousness is as filthy rags to Him. My own self-effort to make myself better was futile. God said the wages of sin is death and that all have sinned and fallen short of the glory of God (Romans 6:23). In God's eyes, sin wasn't fixable without the shedding of blood. Jesus' death and His shed blood paid the penalty for my sins.

But Paul says in Galatians 2:20 that "I am crucified with Christ, nevertheless I live, yet not I, but Christ lives in me." That means when Christ died, I died too. God's solution was death. He knew death was the only answer. That's not only why Jesus had to die, but I had to die too. That's why no one can live the Christian life. The only one who can live a Christian life is Christ.

In Romans 7, Paul gives a wedding analogy. He says when you're married and your spouse dies, you are free to re-marry without becoming an adulterer. He says that, in essence, we were married to the law, sin, and death. But they didn't die—WE died so that we could belong to another—Jesus. The problem is we don't reckon ourselves to be dead.

This same dilemma is what Paul spoke about later in Romans.

That which I want to do (be good) I don't. And that which I don't want to do (be bad) is what I do. Who will rescue me from this body that is subject to death?

The point of Paul's teaching is that death to self is the answer. It is essential. Paul says when Christ died, we died. God doesn't want us to struggle to make our bad life into a good life. He wants to take our life—both bad and good—and exchange it for His life.

The perfect symbolism is baptism. When you are immersed in the water, it symbolizes your death with Christ. Coming up out of the water symbolizes your resurrection to newness of life. The newness is not your old life that was just buried, but a new life—Christ's life in you.

In John 14:1–17:25, Jesus has a lot to say to His disciples about living the Christian life. Most of those four chapters are in red letters—indicating Christ Himself is speaking. He is preparing them for the most significant transition of their life—His presence *with* them to His presence *in* then (the Holy Spirit).

Jesus knew they didn't see the cross coming, nor did they see His death coming, nor His resurrection coming. He knew they would be devastated because they did not anticipate any of those things. He prayed for them (and for us) that they "may be one" with Him as He was one with His Father. Philip asked Jesus to "show us the Father." Jesus answered, "Philip, I have been with you a long time. Do you not know that if you have seen me, you have seen the Father? The Father and I are one" (John 14:8-9).

Jesus wants us to be one with Him, just like He and the Father were one when He walked this earth. That oneness is the single thing that most characterizes His entire ministry. While He was totally human and susceptible to all earthly things, He never ceased to be one with His Father. So, the best definition of the Christian life I've ever read was written by W. Ian Thomas. He said the Christian life is nothing less than "His life then, lived now, by Him, in you." We are to live in oneness with Him.

Oneness with Him requires living a crucified life. You were crucified with Christ, and your life now is His life living in you. You give up your right to yourself and reckon yourself to be dead—but alive in Christ.

I remember thinking, "Okay, I'm crucified." But the next time something happened, I would un-crucify myself and tackle the problem with my self-effort and always fail. I'd tell myself I was going to make God so proud and that I would bring Him glory by my self-effort. I always forgot my self-life was dead.

Paul says again in Colossians 3:1-5,

That since then we have been raised with Christ, set your heart on things above......set your mind on things above not on earthly things. For you died, and your life is now hidden with Christ in God, When Christ, who is your life, appears then you also shall appear with Him in glory. Put to death therefore whatever belongs to your earthly nature....

A typical scenario for me was: There would be a knock on the door. Being crucified, I would yell, "Who is it?" The answer came—"It's Satan, I have a box of temptation for you." That's when

I'd un-crucify myself and always fail. Now when I hear the knock on the door, I simply say, "Jesus, can you get that?" When Jesus gets there, He says, "Who is it?" The answer comes, "It's Satan, and I have a package for Steve White." Jesus says, "He can't come to the door now—he's dead," Jesus then opens the door and says, "But I'm his Lord and Savior, and all authority in heaven and earth has been given to me. So, be gone, Satan, and take that package with you." Meanwhile, I just stay crucified and watch the show. His yoke is easy and His burden is light.

A perfect example of the Christian life is found in Jesus' parable of the vine and the branch (John 15:5). Jesus said, "I am the vine, you are the branch. If you remain in me and I in you, you will bear much fruit. Apart from me you can do nothing." For a branch to have continuous life, it must remain connected to the vine.

Life is in the vine. If a branch is separated from the vine and tries to bear fruit on its own self-effort it will fail. The branch can work out, lift weights, do cardio, eat healthy, get plenty of sunshine, and stay hydrated, but it will always fail. The branch has only one job—to stay connected to the vine. Life is in the vine. Just as having a vital union with the vine is essential to the branch, having a vital union with Christ is critical for the Christian. Our relationship with Him is vital every second of every day. Apart from Him, we can do nothing. Or, alternately stated, anything we do apart from Him (self-effort) will amount to nothing.

Every day, Paul got up and presented himself as a living sacrifice. He asked God to see through his eyes, speak through his mouth, and hear through his ears. He had no will of his own. This is the normal Christian life Watchman Nee speaks about. "Christ in you, the hope of glory" (Colossians 1:27).

In my days of struggling through self-effort to please God, I would always remind myself that, "God doesn't want you to do that." But now that Christ is my life, I listen for His voice. When I get angry in traffic and yell at another driver, I hear Him ask, "Steve, am I still your life?" When I answer yes, He replies, "Well, I don't do that."

When I'm tempted to look at pornography on my laptop, He says, "Steve, am I still your life?" When I answer yes, He says. "Well, I don't look at stuff like that." Gradually I learn what His life in me means and how to let Him live His life through me.

Is it possible for Christians to live a sinless life? I don't know. I do not pay attention to my sin but stay focused on Him. I don't focus on my sin. I acknowledge it, confess it, and refocus on Him, learning as I go what it's like to live His life through me. The branch's only job is to stay connected to the vine.

Now I see myself as an extraterrestrial alien on earth. Paul said our citizenship is in heaven. When I pray, it's like ET phoning home. Jesus didn't die just for my sins; He died to give me His very own life! I can have it now and don't have to wait for heaven. And it's very liberating. I don't have to do anything so I threw my lists away. It's not about performance; it's about relationship.

The Christian life is simply His life then, lived now, by Him, in you.

FOR PERSONAL REFLECTION AND DISCUSSION

- When Paul said, "I am crucified with Christ," what did he mean? What does it mean to you?
- How does Christ live within you?
- What does, "His life then, lived now, by Him, in you" mean to you?

42

Jesus–The Ultimate Game Changer

There have been many inventions over the centuries that have changed the course of history. Perhaps the wheel was the first major invention, and it is still in wide use today. Some other big ones would be the automobile, electricity, the telephone, and let's not forget air conditioning (it's summertime where I live). Looking over my lifetime, I would have to include television, the computer, the internet, and the smart phone.

When I look at my iPhone, I see it has drastically changed my life and the way I do things. I no longer buy a newspaper or read paper books, I text and email more than I call, I no longer have a paper dictionary, need paper maps, or a separate camera, and I do most of my banking on my phone. I no longer need a calculator or a paper encyclopedia or a weather report. I could go on and on about all the ways the iPhone has changed my life.

But the biggest game-changer of all time is Jesus.

Throughout this book, we have been sharing the God we know. We hope people will see a God that more accurately reflects what the Bible says about Him. By seeing God differently, we hope you will think differently, feel differently, and behave differently. We believe knowing God will better meet your needs over time and give you greater peace.

When Jesus was born in a stable in Bethlehem over 2000 years ago, He ushered in a whole new way of Kingdom thinking. He brought new ways to think and see the world. Jesus began His public ministry at about age 30 and preached about the Kingdom of God for three years before His crucifixion. Most of what Jesus taught utterly turned the thoughts of the people that heard Him preach upside down. His whole ministry was about teaching them a new way to think. Just look at some of the things Jesus said:

- The weak will be strong.
- The blind will see.
- The lame will walk.
- The poor will be rich.
- I came not to abolish, but to fulfill.
- You have heard it said, Thou shalt not commit adultery, but I tell you, if you look in lust at another woman you have committed adultery with her already.
- You have heard it said, do not break your oath, but I tell you do not swear an oath at all.
- An eye for an eye, but I tell you do not resist an evil person—turn the other cheek.
- If someone forces you to go a mile, I say go with him two miles
- You have heard it said, hate your enemy, but I tell you to love your enemies, and pray for those who persecute you.
- Do not judge, or you will be judged.
- Why look for a speck in your brother's eye and pay no attention to the plank in your own eye.
- Do unto others what you would have them do to you.
- Seek and you will find, knock and it will be opened unto you.
- And to His disciple Thomas, he said, "Don't you know that if you have seen me, you have seen the Father. The Father and I are One.

We even changed our calendars because of His life. We measure time by B.C. (before Christ) and A.D. (year of our Lord). Jesus took everything they believed and gave them a new way to think about it. He came to change everything. It was no longer just the 10 Commandments—it was the 10 Commandments Plus. Jesus fulfilled the whole of God's laws. And this "Plus" made it apparent no one could keep the laws of Moses. We were all sinners. No one was able to keep the Plus laws.

Jesus performed miracles no one on earth had ever seen before. Jesus raised a man named Lazarus from the dead. He was delayed in arriving at Lazarus' tomb. The man's sisters had hoped Jesus would have arrived earlier so He could have healed Lazarus before he died. But if Jesus had done that, they would only have known Him as Healer. But instead, they would know Him as the Resurrection.

Jesus changed the lives of people. His mother, Mary, was a 14-year-old virgin when she conceived Jesus by the Holy Spirit. She became pregnant with God's Son—do you think it changed her life? Peter was a fisherman and became a fisher of men—do you think he saw things differently? Paul persecuted Christians and then became an Apostle and wrote most of the books in the New Testament—do you think he saw the world differently? For the first time on earth, Jesus showed us that God was a friend who wants a relationship with each one of us.

Jesus said, "I am the Way, the Truth, and the Life." Who was this man who spoke with such authority and claimed to be God Himself? His claims threatened the Chief Priests of the day. His claim to be a King threatened the Roman government. There was only one answer—this man had to die. The crowds chose a thief named Barabbas over Jesus. Pilate, the local Roman governor, washed his hands of the situation and turned Jesus over to be crucified.

Jesus hung on a cross, crucified between two thieves. He was not killed but gave up His spirit voluntarily. And He did it for you! He did it for me! On His shoulders that day, He bore the sins of the whole world. After three days in the grave, He arose. The atonement for all sin had been accomplished; Jesus was alive again forever! Mankind was now reconciled to God. Sins were forgiven, and God's people had been redeemed. Jesus, once and for all, became the Ultimate Game Changer.

It truly is the greatest story ever told. The only thing that remains is—what will you do with this man Jesus? Will you believe He died a substitutionary death for you? Will you accept God's gift of salvation simply by believing that Christ died for you? "Salvation is found in no one else, for there is no other name under heaven given to mankind by which we must be saved" (Acts 4:12).

He alone has the power to help you change your life! A familiar chorus says, "Something beautiful, something good, all my confusion He understood; all I had to offer Him was brokenness and strife, but He made something beautiful of my life! Amen!

I pray the Holy Spirit of God will convict you of your sin, and you will be able to say with assurance, "Jesus died for me."

FOR PERSONAL REFLECTION AND DISCUSSION

- What is the biggest change Jesus brought to earth? Why do you think that?
- How has Jesus changed your life?
- Have you accepted Jesus Christ as your Lord and Savior? If not, please read this book again!

Epilogue

Steve and I hope you have blessed by reading *The God I Know and the Relationship We Need*. So many of the chapters have included our individual encounters with our Father God and that of our spouses, Sherrie and Peter.

We believe there is a need in the United States today for revival. A spiritual revival is simply a religious awakening. Today's world is chaotic with divisions by race, gender, wealth, politics, and age with great unrest about these divisions. We see rioting, looting, arson, and murders of both blacks and police officers. Hatred runs rampant in our society.

Our collective consciences have been seared by radical attacks on the very foundation of our nation and our motto, "In God We Trust." We have removed God from our schools and our lives. We need spiritual revival in our country today. We believe revival will come when people come to know God for who He is. In this book, we have tried to give you a glimpse of God's character, attitude, and personality. He is worth knowing. People need to understand the gifts of salvation and forgiveness of sin, and have a personal relationship with Jesus Christ. God has a master plan for your life.

If you remember nothing else from this book, please remember these four things:

- God wants a personal and loving relationship with you
- God loves you and made provision for the forgiveness of your sins
- Christ's death on the cross paid the full penalty for your sins
- When you come home to God, He will have compassion and run to you with open arms

Come home today and join your life to God. Experience the relationship of your life and treasure the Godhead—Father, Son, and Holy Spirit—as the relationship of your life from this day forward! Amen!

About the Authors

STEVE WHITE has over 30 years of business management experience. He was a partner at Arthur Young (now Ernst & Young) and the partner in charge of the Financial Services Practice in the 13-state East Region. Later, he founded and then sold several consulting firms focused on the Payments industry. Mr. White is a frequent speaker, author, and educator. He served on the faculty at the Pennsylvania Banker's Association School of Banking at Bucknell University. He leads strategic planning sessions in the areas of leadership and vision.

Mr. White is the author of *Please Change Your Mind*, a book about thought management. He was awarded the Rising Star award from his publisher. The book has been endorsed by the Clinical Psychology community. He also wrote *The 11 Things Your Kids Should Know*—a book about changing the next generation. Along with his wife, he has authored two children's books which feature her macro-photography.

Books About Him

JOYCE HILL has a lot of diversity in her professional career. After graduating with a Journalism major/English minor degree from the University of Maryland, she spent seven years as an editor and collateral researcher for a federal government intelligence agency. After finishing her maternity leave, she worked for George Mason University in Fairfax, Virginia, as the chairman's secretary in the School of Business, Finance, and Real Estate academic departments. She reviewed several manuscripts that professors wrote to submit for publication. Her last assignment at George Mason University was to become the manager of the Artificial Intelligence Center under the Department of Computer Science.

For the next nineteen years, she worked as a legal secretary, a patent secretary, and a patent paralegal for Pillsbury Madison and Sutro (now Pillsbury Madison Shaw Pittman), a national law firm. Her last professional endeavor was as a realtor for Long and Foster, where she spent four years until she and her husband retired to Lancaster County, PA.

They both attended and graduated from the C.S. Lewis Institute Fellows Program, Years One and Two. She has taught Bible studies in her community for the past four years, and she and her husband are part of a forthcoming church plant in Lancaster County, PA. This is her first published work.

How This Book Happened

One of the miracles of our book is how it came to be written in the first place. Steve and I went to Sherwood High School in Sandy Spring, MD and graduated in the Class of '65. He was our star athlete, and I edited our high school's magazine, *The Twigs*. When graduation day came, we celebrated as a class and went our separate ways. Fifty-five years later, our paths crossed on Facebook. Steve had written two books by then—*Please Change Your Mind* and *The 11 Things Your Kids Should Know,* both of them based on the concept of thought management. (I recommend both of these books for good, solid Christian reading.)

After I read the first book, I casually asked Steve when he was going to write his next book. His response was to ask me to be a co-author on this book! We wrote the manuscript and hired an amazing Christian literary agent, Keith Carroll, who promptly suggested we rewrite the book with a focus on God as our Father.

We started this project around Memorial Day, 2020. I am an editor and had never written a book. Yet, the Lord continually gave both of us ideas and themes that a non-believer or a new believer might ask about being born again and living the Christian life. Some of the chapters literally wrote themselves. During the writing of this book, God worked mightily in our individual lives, bringing healing to both of us. We could not have done this without the prayers and encouragement of our spouses whose ideas and suggestions made this book richer than it was.